Edie from Elizabeth
Christmas 1972

My love to a companion on
the journey.

Enjoy the Journey

··{ *Lionel A. Whiston* }··

ENJOY
the
JOURNEY

WORD BOOKS, Publisher
Waco, Texas

Contents

Preface

Where is the joy that once I knew
When first I found the Lord?

In these few words the poet echoes the unspoken question in the hearts of all too many Christians. But for many others, it is not a matter of having known joy and then lost it. For these men and women, God has never been real; serving him, therefore, cannot possibly be exciting.

This book is the story of discovering God's great love, of our response to him, and of the exciting fellowship that results. All things become new: the sacraments, the Bible, our relationships with God and man. Joy is being constantly renewed.

Following Paul's pattern of starting with the announcement of the Good News (the kerygma) and following with teaching about practical matters (the didache), I have divided the book into two parts.

Literally thousands of people—friends and families, parishioners, and those I have encountered in retreats and conferences—have contributed to this book. Wherever I go, I stand amazed at people's degree of commitment and loyalty to their Master, regardless of cost. What I have written mirrors the insights and ideas I have received from them.

I am equally impressed by their search for the reality of God and for meaning in life. Such a search is integral to man's nature. On every hand I am confronted by the questions this search inspires. Here are answers, in part, and guidelines for continued quest.

LIONEL A. WHISTON

Wrentham, Massachusetts

PART I

··{ *1* }··

First Things First

The first piece of property my wife and I owned was an unpretentious summer cottage by a lake. Not a door in that cottage would close tightly. I kept promising myself that someday I would remedy the situation—saw and plane a bit here, put on a "dutchman" there, get the doors to fit snugly.

But one summer passed and another rolled around, and still I had done nothing about the doors.

That year we planned to be away for a week, and the thought came that we should lend someone the cottage rather than let it stand idle. Sam Owens's name leaped to mind. Sam had a large family and little or no money for vacations. When I asked if he and his family would like to spend a week at the cottage, he jumped at the chance.

A day or two later it occurred to me that Sam, a carpenter, might feel obligated to do some work around the place since he was getting it "for free." I went to him and said sternly, "Sam, no carpenter work while you are at the camp!" At first he demurred, but finally he said, "Okay, Lee."

When we returned from our week away, a happy thank-you note from the Owenses was there to greet us. As we settled in to the cottage, I soon became aware that all the doors now closed easily.

"That son of a gun!" I exclaimed. "I told Sam not to do any work around here. I might have known he would."

Every door in the cottage fit exactly into its frame. It was such a perfect job that not even a careful examination revealed where the wood had been planed or added to.

The next time I saw Sam I really lit into him. "You faithfully promised not to do any carpenter work in the house, and then you went and straightened all the doors. You know, Sam, all I wanted you to do was relax and enjoy yourself."

He seemed puzzled. "But, Lee, I didn't touch the doors. I kept my promise."

"But before you came, not a door in the house would close. And now they all do."

Sam's face lit up with understanding. "Oh, I see what you're talking about. The second day I was there I was walking up the driveway and noticed that the ridgepole was out of line, sagging in the middle. So I got out my automobile jack, lifted up the center sill of the cottage, and slid a couple of flat stones between the beam and the foundation. When I straightened out the main sill, everything else must have fallen into place."

So it is with life. Once our relationship to God is right, everything else falls into place. Like the North Star for a navigator, God is the point from which we take our guidelines. As the main theme of a classical symphony provides the basis for the minor themes and variations, holding all together in order and harmonious beauty, so faith in God provides the theme that draws the faculties and energies of life into a purposeful whole.

In a life centered around the self, without reference to God, nothing really fits; everything is awry. Yet throughout history men have placed themselves at the center of the universe. This is as true today as ever, and we hear the question asked again and again: "Who am I?"

The answer to that question is "Legion," the name the demoniac applied to himself (Mark 5:9). In different situations we are different selves—"Today so safe and brave; tomorrow too weak to try." Man needs God, the unchanging source of selfhood in whom we find our being. It is God who sets our feet upon a rock. The question is not "who we are," but "whose we are."

I once met a woman who was torn apart by the desire to please the important people in her life. In her anxiety to be a good wife and insure a happy marriage, she strained constantly to please her husband. She was so afraid of not being a good mother that she was forever overreaching in doing things for her children.

As for her house, it must be immaculate at all times. And, wanting to stand well with her neighbors, she spent many hours planning and carrying out social activities.

When I met her, she seemed to wear a thin outer shell of efficiency, but inside there was a bundle of raw nerves. By trying to be all things to all people, she had reached the point where she was ready to break into pieces.

Fortunately, she was able to see and acknowledge what had happened, and her near desperation had made her ready for an inner change. She prayed, "God, I give my marriage into your keeping. I will stop trying to make it successful. I will stop trying to please my husband at every turn. And I give my children to you. I've carried them constantly in my mind, waiting on them till I was utterly exhausted. My house has been my god. I have sought to please my neighbors more than you. Dear God, I give all these over to you. From now on I will seek to obey only you."

The weeks that followed brought relaxation to that woman in her family and community relations. She was truly a new person.

It is pathetic to see men and women torn by conflicting goals. Some try to cater to different groups; chameleon-like, they adopt the coloration of various viewpoints and values. Others are torn by the desire for status, power, or security. Diverse authorities vie with each other for the control of their lives.

What a relief it is to find one's central authority in God! What joy, to see conflicting forces drawn into a unified purpose! When we put God first, the rest of life assumes its proper place (Matt. 6:33). All too often we try to adjust the various "doors," all unconscious of the fact that "the main beam has sagged."

The decision to put God first not only provides a clear focus for a life, but it also heightens the contrast between good and evil, and *between the good and the less good*.

Usually we know full well when we have chosen evil over good, for here the issue is clear-cut. When a Christian is faced with evil, there is only one thing for him to do: turn his back on it and forsake it. However, difficulties often arise when we are called on to choose between two goods—between loyalties and situations that both seem to offer worthwhile goals.

Ned was a brilliant businessman, confident and skilled and widely recognized as a leader among men. His subordinates admired his decisions and relied on his judgment. But Ned was compulsively driven by perfectionism. He simply must not fail his company, his board of directors, and the stockholders. Most of all, he must not compromise the goals he had set for himself.

Ned's deep-seated conscientiousness had its origins in his childhood training. His parents had expected a perfect performance in everything he attempted. No matter how splendid the report card he brought home from school, they commented there was room for improvement. No matter how neat he kept his room or his basement workshop, it was never quite good enough.

Because he was unable to reach the impossible goals set for him, Ned came to feel that he was a disappointment to his parents and that, therefore, they did not love him. For years he tried to win their affection and earn their approval. This pattern, striving for perfection and fearing failure, carried over full-blown into his adult life, both in his personal and business relationships.

At heart, however, Ned longed to be known as a warm, loving, Christian person. Often he would try to break the chains of his efficiency so that he could relate to his fellow workers on a personal level. Always these attempts came to nothing, for the fear remained that if he truly became a friend to others, he would imperil the perfectionism to which he was compulsively driven.

While the desires of his heart did battle with the demands of his head, Ned suffered. His capacity for love remained hidden, but the conflict brought sleepless nights, periodic bouts with asthma, and the threat of a complete breakdown.

At last the dilemma became so agonizing that Ned prayed in despair, "God, take away my drive for perfection! Melt the habits of years and let me be an ordinary mortal. I don't want to be a machine; I want to be a human being, a channel of your love and compassion."

In his brokenness, Ned found immediate release. By faith he put his business into the hands of God. His motivation changed, for no longer did he seek to be efficient, but only to do God's will daily. Into his life came a new emphasis—an emphasis on human values which enhanced the significance of others, drew out their skills, and built friendship and freedom into Ned's relationships with subordinates. Imagination, inventiveness, and loyalty replaced efficiency, admiration, and perfectionism.

Ned's discovery was not unlike that which countless others have made when they came to the end of self-effort. It is easy to replace the worship of God with the worship of some idea or program of our own making.

Such a substitute for God can be almost anything—a career, homemaking, community activities, even Bible study and church meetings. It was quite a shock to me to discover when I was in my late thirties that I was spending so much time in church work that I was neglecting fellowship with my wife and children. Night after night I was away from home, unavailable to my family. Some mornings I would bury myself in the Bible while my wife struggled to get the children off to school on time.

In my younger years I had been an introvert who tended to withdraw from encounter with others. It was a serious denial of God's primacy in my life that, instead of risking rejection or mediocre accomplishment, I did the work of ten people rather than set ten people to work. Of course, deep inside me, as I was to see later, was the prideful thought that I could do the work better.

Deep inner conflict and ill health—both physical and mental—brought me to the place where I gave up struggling to be a successful pastor, adequate in every situation. I accepted my limitations and my humanity and acknowledged them to God and man. "God," I cried out, "I've tried and tried. I can't do it. I quit. Will you take over?"

With this capitulation came the recognition and acceptance of my weakness and inadequacy, but there immediately followed the inrush of God's strength and leading, as I determined to seek to do God's will no matter how often I failed.

Paul says we have this treasure in earthen vessels (2 Cor. 4:7). The humanity we tend to deny is the very bridge that ties us to others. Our earthiness makes us kin to our fellows. When we see and accept ourselves as nothing more than pots of clay, we suddenly make the discovery that God's treasure (his Spirit, his power, and his love) is poured into these vessels of ours to overflowing, so that wherever we go his love reaches into the lives of others.

The focus of our thinking is transferred from our earthiness to our being channels of his riches. We see ourselves as recipients and dispensers of his grace. With a leap of imagination, we no longer see men after the flesh (2 Cor. 5:16), but as containers of the treasures of God. And we see all men in terms of their divine potential.

This, too, makes brothers of all men and binds us, flesh and spirit, humanity and divinity, to one another.

Striving for perfection often brings tension and fear in its wake. The prayer for perfection can easily become the prelude to a fall: "God, don't let me slip this time." "Help me not to make a mistake." "Don't let me fail as I did yesterday." We also pass fear on to others, as when a mother says to her little child, "Now, don't drop that dish. I just know you are going to drop it if you aren't careful!"

Such prayers and suggestions are self-centered, focusing on our desire to be perfect or blameless. Moreover, they tend to become self-fulfilling realities. And anyway, what good would it accomplish in the world if I, for instance, became a "perfect" Lee Whiston? My very perfection would make me insufferable and a threat to my fellow-men!

But the moment I accept myself as one who frequently fails, knowing full well that my motivation is to do God's will in each day-by-day situation as it arises, then I can relax in God's love and know that I am his. He loves me whether I fail or not.

A Dennis the Menace cartoon shows the little rascal kneeling beside his bed, saying his prayers. "Well, God, I goofed again!"

What a sensible attitude! When we are free to say this, we can accept God's forgiveness, forgive ourselves, and plunge into the next task.

Christians who are trapped in the vicious "perfectionism-failure" cycle miss out on the joyous and released abandon of a life given over to God. One can be so preoccupied with being a good father or husband or churchman, doing all the right things, polishing one's character until it glows, making the job or home or church into the ultimate, that he never learns how to "sit loose" and "cast his cares on the Lord."

In a life crowded with anxiety and worries, striving for adequacy or success, compulsion for perfection, there is not much room for the presence of God. Trust in God really means to *trust God* and not put one's ultimate trust in his own ability to take care of his own life.

Questions for Study

1. Recall some instance when ill health may have resulted from the failure to put God first.

2. How has the desire to be efficient or perfect occasionally hindered you from a warm relationship with God or your fellow-man? What are the personality factors which lead to the compulsion always to be right?

3. There are times when one is more eager to impress people than to obey God. What experience have you had along this line?

4. Discuss to what extent your security depends on being successful as a spouse, a parent, a homemaker, or on the job. How can you place your security more firmly in God?

5. Tell of a situation or situations in your life when putting God first has enabled you to do your tasks in more efficient and relaxed ways.

··{ 2 }··
God's Love
Unique and Personal

Did you ever try substituting your own name for a general term in a familiar Bible verse? It can be an illuminating experiment.

For example, read John 3:16–17 like this: "For God so loved John Anderson that he gave his only Son, that John Anderson believing in him should not perish but have eternal life. For God sent his Son into the world, not to condemn John Anderson, but that John Anderson might be saved."

The Bible suddenly comes alive when we see this great love of God coming directly and personally to each one of us. "By his stripes, I Susan Jones am healed." "Fear not, Sue, I have called you by name. . . . I will be with you, Sue, wherever you go."

We never truly experience the love of God until we know for certain that it is for us. Of course, it circumscribes God's love to think of it as meant only for us,

21

rather than embracing all mankind. Nevertheless, if God's love is to be real to you, it must have your name on it.

If this concept seems odd to you, imagine yourself in a different situation. You are standing on the shore of a lake on a moonlit night. The moonbeams come over a golden bridge of reflections directly to your feet, and you say, "It shines for me. It's my moon."

Naturally, you know full well that the person standing next to you can have the same experience and say the same words, but this does not deny the experience as uniquely yours.

God's call to us to serve him through Christian action comes in precisely the same highly individual way. Two people watch a television documentary. The camera focuses on dark-skinned, starving children. Emaciated bodies and bloated bellies show the result of man's insensitivity to his fellows. One of the viewers says, "I must do something about this." The other adds, "God is tapping me on the shoulder, too. What can we do together to help alleviate this suffering?" Here are God's call and man's response, as each person hears God speaking to him personally.

God loves and plans for mankind as if each person were the only one on earth. Parents get some inkling of this in relation to their children. Their full affection and concern are given to their first baby. But when the second is born, they do not say, "How unfortunate that we can love each of our children only half as much, now that there are two." No! Each child is loved with a total love.

The impressive aspect of God's love is that it is not diminished as it is distributed among many people. God does not give each of us on this planet one three-billionth part of his affection. He loves every one of us with all of his concern. If you were the only person alive, God's love for you would be no more intimate or powerful.

The creation is incredible in its diversity and lack of duplication. God never made two leaves alike. Even in the simplest forms of life, visible only under powerful microscopes, there are minuscule variations.

A photographer once conducted an experiment with snowflakes. He took pictures of forty thousand snowflakes and viewed them under a microscope. Every flake was symmetrical, intricate and delicate, a perfectly harmonious design, but the photographer found no two that were exactly alike.

So it is with humanity; no two persons are identical. And as we are every one of us different from everyone else who ever lived, God loves us in a special way. He says, "Before I formed you in the womb I knew you, and before you were born I consecrated you" (Jer. 1:5, RSV). He plans for each of us differently, according to our needs, circumstances, and potential.

This quality of God's love for each of us is mirrored in our love for others. A mother holds her child tightly in her arms and says, "No baby was ever loved like this one." Then, perhaps, she wonders if that is a foolish thing to say since every parent could say the same thing. But it is true. A parent's love for his child is something special for that child alone. It is a love that can never be duplicated.

In the same way a man may confidently say to the woman he loves, "No girl was ever loved the way I love you." Where real love is concerned, such a statement is always true because every love relationship is unique.

We have this experience in varying degrees whenever we come to appreciate a person, or even an object or an activity. God looked at the world he had made and said, "It is good." Of his people, he said, "You are my people, bound to me with an everlasting love." This same love, reflected in the experience of a man, expresses itself as joy in his work, satisfaction in what he creates, delight and pride in his home and country, and deep, unique affection for every person he has come to love.

How steadfast is God's love for us! He always takes the initiative, believing in us when others have lost faith in us, and even when we have lost faith in ourselves. He affirms us when we are most uncertain of our worth. He loves us when we are most unlovely.

We would be poor indeed if God's love for us depended on our love for him. But the reverse is true: "In this is love, not that we loved God but that he loved us" (1 John 4:10, RSV). The psalms speak repeatedly of a God who hears, cares, and strengthens his people. How often I have felt lonely or unworthy of love, but when I have come to God, he has heard me and loved me. I can depend on the faithfulness, constancy, and steadfastness of the God I know through Jesus Christ.

This love is unconditional, flowing freely toward all men regardless of their behavior or performance. Love is God's ultimate weapon. It is by means of this "weapon" that God draws men to him, builds his Kingdom on earth, and assures the triumph of right over wrong. Jesus' life was the embodiment and demonstration of this kind of love. He was and is God's final word, his last resort, his ultimate act of faith.

There was nothing passive about the kind of love Jesus

practiced and revealed. "If anyone forces you to go one mile," he said, "go with him two miles." Far from being a mere legalistic command, this was symbolic of a way of life and a depth of love that frequently goes *beyond* the second mile.

Imagine a scene in Nazareth, two thousand years ago. Roman soldiers often marched through that village, which was located on the main route from Syria to Egypt. As they approached, the news would spread quickly among boys playing in the streets and men working nearby that another Roman cohort was on its way. People would scatter, hiding wherever they could because they were well aware of the Roman law which allowed any soldier to commandeer anyone he chose to carry his baggage a thousand paces. It was a case of obey or be punished.

Inevitably the soldiers would get their hands on some of the youths and angrily sling heavy bags onto their shoulders, snarling curses and even adding injury to insult with a prod of the javelin. They demanded obedience to the letter of the Roman law, and frequently when the mile was passed, they would illegally demand that the youths go even further.

In our imagination we can picture Jesus returning to the village, noticing a soldier with a heavy burden, walking straight up to him, and offering to carry his load. The weary soldier, surprised by this evidence of good will, suspiciously accepts the offer. The two fall into easy conversation.

Jesus might ask the soldier questions about himself, his family back home, the countries he has visited and then tell about his own brothers and sisters and of the fine carpenter work his father does. The minutes and the miles pass by.

Suddenly the Roman, becoming aware of how far they have walked, says, "Hey, boy, you've come five or six miles, far more than you had to."

"That's all right; I'll go to the top of the next hill."

When he returns home, Jesus is greeted by the sneers of his fellows. "Why did you offer to carry that evil dog's load? What are you? A collaborator? A Roman-lover?"

In his day, when Roman soldiers oppressed the Jews in their native land, when tax collectors were hated, when lepers were outcasts, and when harlots were publicly despised, Jesus personified the love of God toward these unwanted people. It was a love that took the initiative and knew no limit. It was a love that involved Jesus himself, whatever the cost to him.

As human beings, we tend to *react* to other people, relating most easily to those who respond to us and avoiding or resenting those who treat us indifferently. But God never *reacts*. He *responds*, steadfastly and constantly, with an infinite capacity for caring and compassion, regardless of what our attitudes may be.

The life of Jesus was both profound and very simple. He embodied the great love of God and expressed it in warm relationships with his Father and with his fellowmen, especially those in need. His life was like a reservoir from which good will overflowed to God's other children. Each of us can say, "This love of God is personally mine through Jesus Christ, his Son."

When we begin to sense, respond to, and appropriate this enabling love of God, we soon discover that it is a far cry from what often passes for love on a human level. There are many loves that cripple and constrict human growth, inculcate fear, and deny the potential that is in embryo in every man. Possessive, manipulative loves are perverted, for they thwart and diminish man. The genius of the love of God is that instead of stifling our individuality, it preserves our integrity, enriches our personality, and releases the potential that God has implanted in each of us.

To me this is the meaning of Jesus' words to Simon. " 'You are Simon son of John. You shall be called Cephas' (that is, Peter, the Rock)" (John 1:42, NEB). Bystanders undoubtedly took this opportunity to snicker at Jesus' expense. "Simon? That big blabbermouth? He promises, but never delivers. Imagine calling him a rock! Why, even an idiot would know better than that."

But Jesus had discerned deep within this man a strength and stability unseen by others. Instead of delivering a lecture on the foolishness of boasting, Jesus gave Simon Peter an awareness of the person he could become.

Over and over again I have seen biblical incidents re-enacted in various ways. For example, the story of how Jesus commanded the paralytic to take up his pallet and walk, enabling him to carry what for years had carried him. I saw this miracle take place in the emotional life of a woman who had come to a conference seeking help. For years she had been immersed in self-pity. Suddenly she became aware of the needs of others. Her sensitivity, turned inward, had been her protective cave, yet in it she had found only unhappiness. Turned outward, it became her joyous witness to the love of God. Thus our latent capabilities are summoned to consciousness by Christ who believes in that inner strength within each of us.

God has shown himself to us in Jesus, so that, knowing him, each of us may see the person he can become. "To all who did receive him, to those who have yielded him their allegiance, he gave the right to become children of God, . . . the offspring of God himself" (John 1:12–13, NEB).

The process by which this takes place is a paradox. The self that we cherish must die, as a seed is buried in the soil, in order that a new and more abundant life may result. To hold onto one's self, to rely wholly on our own abilities, or to seek to build ourselves up will result in eventual frustration or failure. To lose ourselves for the cause of Christ and his Kingdom is to discover a new self, the real self.

We see this illustrated in the man who risks his life for a noble cause, even in the attitude of the team player who throws himself wholeheartedly into a game, losing his identity in the process. Paul put it this way: "I have been crucified with Christ; it is no longer I who live, but Christ who lives in me; and the life I now live in the flesh I live by faith in the Son of God, who loved me and gave himself for me" (Gal. 2:20, RSV).

God does not wish men to be puppets, robots, or ditto marks. He encourages the abandon of men who are committed to building a new world of brotherhood—seeking, aiming, blundering, being hurled back, trying again and yet again. In Paul's words, "Hard-pressed on every side, we are never hemmed in; bewildered, we are never at our wits' end; hunted, we are never abandoned to our fate; struck down, we are not left to die. Wherever we go we carry death with us in our body, the death that Jesus died, that in this body also life may reveal itself, the life that Jesus lives" (2 Cor. 4:8–10, NEB).

In a world of increasing depersonalization, God always

meets us on a person-to-person basis so that each of us may say, "God is *my* Father. Jesus is *my* Savior and Friend." In a day of credibility gaps, broken faith, and smoldering hostility, Christ lives within us, helping us to live out truth as we relate in outgoing friendliness to our fellows. We then become the embodiment of his constant, steadfast love, ever initiating, ever outgoing.

In a computer age of punch-card uniformity, God offers to each of us a unique relationship both with him and with our fellow-men—a relationship that is kept fresh in Christ. Our society is one of power, status, and struggle, yet in the midst of it all comes this amazing paradox—in losing we find, in spending we save, in dying we live.

Questions for Study

1. Mention several passages of Scripture which you have personalized by insertion of your own name. How did this give them a special meaning to you?

2. Recall an occasion when you have felt the love of God personally directed toward you. What induced this experience? Can you remember any incidents which seemed to trigger this response in you?

3. Is it easier for you to go second miles with people you like? Why? Tell of an occasion when you went a second mile with someone you did not like. Could this be done sometimes as a duty fulfillment? Was it done in love? What happened as a result?

4. What is the difference between "reacting" and "responding" to other people? Describe some relationship or

situation where reaction should be changed to response.

5. How would you describe what the love of God means to you when telling it (a) to a young child, (b) to an adult?

6. What factors in your life tend to make you feel like a "thing" or a "machine"? What tends to make you feel like a person? How can you diminish the first and increase the second? What part does acceptance play in this transformation?

..{3}..

The Power to Become

The voice coming over the telephone wire was full of anxiety. "Will you come and see Florence and can you do it today?"

Of course I could and did go to that home. When I reached it, I realized why he was so urgent. His wife lay gravely ill, and it was quite a shock to hear her say, "Pastor, I haven't long to live, and I have never been baptized. Would you be willing to baptize me?"

"Of course," I replied.

"Right here in this room?"

"Why, yes. I can instruct you and baptize you right here. But I want to baptize you into life, not into death. Whether it is to be in heaven or on earth, God wants you to live."

Florence told me that five years before she had had a very serious operation for cancer. Now the cancer had returned and spread. X-rays revealed dark, telltale areas. Worse still, her pain was becoming unbearable.

As she spoke, I kept praying silently, asking God to help me meet her needs. It appeared that this brave woman's chief concern was for her husband and her aged mother, who depended greatly upon her. I assured her that Christ could come into her life and help her, right there, as she lay in her bed.

Wanting her to make a complete commitment of her life to God, I suggested that she place her arms on top of the quilt and turn her hands palms upward with her fingers relaxed. Then I asked her if she would, in her imagination, place into her hands everything that was troubling her—her husband, who would miss her sorely; her mother, so dependent upon her; her own dread of the ever-increasing pain which she knew might be in store; and the entire future with all its uncertainties.

Finally she spoke of her own personality and the sharp tongue and cutting words that had often been her undoing. Her conscience was troubled over the many people she had hurt. These feelings of guilt she also placed into her cupped hands through the power of imagination. I asked her to think in silence for a minute or two. Was there anything else that should be put there?

"Now," I said, "turn your hands over, and as you do so, give everything over to God. Drop it all, as it were, into the ocean of God's love."

As she complied, I continued: "Your husband is in God's hands. You have taken your hands off him completely and entrusted him to God. Your mother, too, is in God's safekeeping. And the hurts you have caused others, both intentionally and inadvertently, have all been forgiven. God will undoubtedly lead you to make some restitutions. Your illness also is in God's hands; he will be with you through the pain, and he will bless your suffering. The future is God's, and you are now completely willing for him to work out his will."

A light came into Florence's eyes, and an expression of deep peace shone from her face.

"Now turn your hands over again," I suggested. "Into your empty, upturned hands, even at this very moment, God is pouring his peace, his power, and his love."

She lay silently for a few moments, and I was acutely conscious that she literally sensed the love of God flowing through her hands into her whole being. Two or three minutes later, she opened her eyes. Yes, there were tears, but there was also radiance in her expression.

"I would never have dreamed this could happen," she said. "I know that God is with me, and whatever takes place will be all right. God will take care of my loved ones, and he will take care of me."

In so short a time, a miracle had taken place. Florence had experienced in her heart the healing presence of the loving Christ.

"Now, Florence," I said, "you asked if I would baptize you right here. Of course I will, but I believe God would like you to be baptized in the church. God rewards people of great faith; he honors a daring spirit. If God heals you, will you walk down the aisle of the church to be baptized? Will you, right now, tell him that you believe he can heal you and that he will heal you?"

Again there were moments of silence. Then, thoughtfully, she said, "I believe he can heal me . . . I believe he has started to do it now." Together we had a prayer of thanksgiving. Healing had already begun.

During the next several weeks, fifteen or twenty of us

in prayer groups, and others in the congregation, surrounded Florence with prayer.

The day after my visit, she was out of bed. Still bowed
in pain, she did her housework leaning on a chair which
she pushed about in front of her with great difficulty. The
pain continued unabated for two weeks, and then it began to ease.

A month later, x-rays showed that the dark patches of
disease were much lighter. Eight weeks later, they were
almost gone. Florence announced that she was ready to be
baptized.

"Would you like someone to take your arm as you
walk down the aisle next Sunday?" I asked.

She hesitated a moment and then said, "No, I'm going to
lean on the arm of God."

There were few dry eyes in the church that Sunday
morning as Florence walked forward, straight as a soldier,
with confident bearing. When I placed my hands upon
her head in the rite of baptism, the presence of the Holy
Spirit seemed to be felt throughout the entire congregation.

Two weeks later a friend remarked, "I can't get over
the change in Florence Bullard."

Thinking that he meant the physical healing, I said,
"Yes, it's wonderful to see her out and around again." To
which he countered, "I don't mean that. It's her disposi-
tion. It used to be that she never came to my office without
saying caustic and bitter things about her neighbors. But
lately she always has something good to say. I've never
seen such a change in a person."

Florence lived on in good health for four more years, a
witness to God's love and healing.

The renewing, restoring power of God is everywhere at work. If I scratch my finger, it starts to heal immediately. If a branch of a plant is broken, scar tissue forms and new growth appears elsewhere. When a lie is told, conscience goes to work, seeking to reestablish truth. When there is a rift in a friendship, unhappiness sets in until the relationship is restored. The love of God always seeks to redeem all of his creation, to make and keep it whole.

The universe is on the side of right and health. Tagore, the Indian poet, said, "Everything lifts up strong hands after perfection." Plants reach up to the light of the sun; scientists search for knowledge; diseased bodies form antibodies to fight infection and restore health; tortured minds battle for peace by blocking out terrifying experiences; sin-burdened souls long for forgiveness. Everywhere the Spirit of God is at work, making life whole.

This power of God is not fixed or static. It does not put life to rights the way one lifts a stick to an upright position with the admonition, "Stay there!" It is a dynamic, restorative love, constantly creating and recreating. God sees the person that each of us can become, and having envisioned this, he seeks to recreate us, moment by moment, in order to fulfill his perfect will in us. Tomorrow must be built on today, and the next morrow on that, if we are to move forward toward his perfect will. Each tomorrow can be a miracle of newness.

What is more, God accommodates his plans to our human frailties. Life is an infinite series of new beginnings because God's love is an infinite series of forgivenesses and accommodations of his plan to our limitations and failures. Lovingly, patiently, with eagerness and faith, he presents to us each moment a new plan that is possible of fulfillment, beginning at the place where we now stand. We come to him confidently because he always has faith in us and for us. This is the mystery and wonder of the indwelling presence of God in Christ. This is what we mean when we claim "the power to become" (John 1:12).

His love is in us and around us, lifting us up and molding us into the persons we can become in him. This healing, or being made whole, does not take place because of what we do but because something is being done to us. Henry Drummond observed that the great verbs of the New Testament are in the passive voice: we do not "born ourselves," we *are born* again. Paul does not say, "Transform yourself," but *"Be ye transformed."* We are surrounded by a divine initiative, constantly invading our lives. As we respond, divine love makes and remakes us, a process we could not achieve on our own, and, moreover, a process that does not end.

The world is shot through and through with the restorative power of love. We read of Jesus, "As many as touched him were made whole" (Mark 6:56, KJV). John writes of the river of the water of life that is for the healing of nations, and affirms that the living Christ dwells in our midst "making all things new" (Rev. 21:5; 22:1–2).

There are, however, *two* aspects necessary to healing. One is God's gracious power, which we have been discussing. The other is faith, and this is where man's part comes in as he responds to the power of God.

Florence Bullard is a perfect example of faith. In spite of adverse circumstances, in spite of bleak prospects, she believed. In her case, the depth of faith was truly remarkable, for Florence was a trained nurse and well aware of her own medical prognosis. Humanly speaking, there was no hope, yet she projected faith. There is a creative power in faith like this. All around us are examples of things that "simply could not happen," and yet happened when people believed.

The faith of four men was a prelude to Jesus' healing of the paralytic (Mark 2:5). To the woman in the crowd he said, "Your faith has made you well" (Luke 8:48, RSV). Jesus placed great emphasis on faith and commended it even when as small as a grain of mustard seed.

It is important not only that persons themselves have faith, but also that others have faith for them. We have seen the leap of faith that Florence Bullard took for herself. Let us consider the need of faith for one another.

Lack of faith is obvious, and often devastating. A father says of his son, "I can't trust that boy; he drives like a demon. I know he'll have a smash-up." The expectancy of an accident only increases the likelihood of its happening. A mother sends her child out to play with the warning, "If you come home with another cold, I'll never forgive you," thus creating an emotional situation in which resistance is lowered and viruses thrive.

Evidence of the positive and negative aspects of faith is found not only in cases of physical health and ill health. Learning, too, is powerfully affected by the climate of faith in which students operate. A wealth of psychological data has been accumulated showing that the best learning takes place in situations where it is confidently anticipated. It is not so much a question of the teacher's skill or the student's innate ability; what seems to make the greatest difference is faith.

Despite our knowledge of all these circumstances, we perpetually fall into the trap of inviting disaster through lack of faith. Parents in their dealings with their children; trustees planning a financial campaign; workers starting on a difficult job; students facing a new term; labor and management meeting to negotiate a new contract—in virtually every human relationship the mood of fear and pessimism settles in, creating an atmosphere which is an open invitation to failure and frustration. Across the centuries comes the voice of Jesus as a clarion call to faith. He says to us as he said to the centurion who sought healing for his servant, "Go; be it done for you *as you have believed*" (Matt. 8:13, RSV, italics mine).

This story illustrates the power of both the presence and the absence of faith.

One of my parishioners, a woman named Lucille, worked in a laundry. One day her hand was caught in a machine, her arm squeezed and twisted. I saw her the next day in the hospital. Her hand was drawn into such a hideous shape that I could not bear to look at it. She must have sensed my revulsion, for she hid her hand under a sheet.

Even as I prayed with Lucille that her hand would be healed, I was conscious of that disfigured hand. My lips voiced positive faith, but my imagination focused on the negative, and the latter had the greater power under the circumstances!

When I got home I had a session with myself. What was the use of my praying if all I could see was a crippled hand? What use was I, a pastor, to Lucille if I pictured malformity while praying for wholeness?

The thought came to me: "You've got to see that hand whole. You've got to see it in your mind's eye as being entirely well." But every time I thought of Lucille, I envisioned the crippled shape and felt hopeless about it.

Then came the challenge. Would I be willing to begin training my imagination so that with eyes closed I could see her bruised hand healed, as perfect as the other? For six weeks, three times a day, I sat alone for five minutes, imagining that Lucille sat before me, stretching out her two hands. I looked at each of them and tried to see both well and normal. For the first week or two I made no apparent progress; then I began to see the injured hand completely well for a split second. Finally, after six weeks, I could see both outstretched hands as normal and healthy.

Meanwhile, I had been calling on Lucille in her apartment from time to time. I had prayed and sought to bring strength, knowing in my heart that I was failing her. But when the day came that I was able to envision her hand as well, my entire being was filled with faith for her healing.

That day I told Lucille all that had gone before, beginning with my shock and revulsion (which she admitted she had sensed), my six weeks of discipline and prayer, and now my ability to see her hands made whole. I asked her to stretch out both hands. Taking them into my hands, I looked from her eyes to her hands and back again. "Lucille," I said, "I see both hands alike, well and whole. I know God will bring healing. Let us thank him."

Then I prayed, "Father, I thank you that in your heart and in my eyes you have already made Lucille's hand whole again. I thank you for the miracle of healing. We claim it together and trust you to complete it in the flesh."

Within ten days the hand was 85 percent healed, and the complete healing came after several months.

The right attitude of mind is of tremendous importance in all phases of life. There is untold power in creative and disciplined imagination. Dr. Maxwell Maltz tells of a test he made with a group of basketball players. He asked each of them to shoot a specified number of baskets, noting the percentage of successful shots. He then divided the players into three equal groups, and asked the first group not to touch a basketball for three weeks. The second group was asked to shoot baskets half an hour a day for three weeks. Each member of the third group was asked to relax in a comfortable chair for half an hour a day, imagining that he was shooting baskets. When the shots missed, he was to correct his shooting in his mind's eye. He was to concentrate on getting the ball into the basket with each shot.

At the end of the three-week period, the young men were brought onto the basketball floor again and their skill tested in comparison with their former achievements. The group that had done nothing showed no improvement. The group that had practiced showed 23 percent improvement. The third group showed a 20 percent improvement, almost as much as that of the players who went out and practiced physically on the basketball floor!

Whenever I reflect on such wonderful physical and spiritual healings as I have described in this chapter, I am reminded that God's great desire to work out his plans does not necessarily mean that all of our prayers made in total faith will be answered in the ways we may have wished. I have prayed, and I am sure the reader has prayed, with the most sincere commitment, and yet the loved one has not been restored to health or even to life as we know it here on earth.

It is not for us to know whom God will heal, or when. But it is our privilege to align ourselves with God's healing power and surround people with God's love and power to make whole. It is like a game. We may not always win on the "scoreboard," but we have won in the great game of life whenever with strong prayer and faith we have enlisted God's power to do battle with the forces of disease and sin. The results of our prayers and faith we leave with God.

Florence Bullard was healed in body and spirit, but the time came when God took her to himself. The significant thing is that although her death came in four years, she did not die sick. Her whole being during those four years was transformed. There was a very short period of terminal illness during which time the glow of faith on her face and the transformation of her personality bore witness to God's continued victory in her life. And it is possible for every one of us to experience the complete wholeness of spirit that God has in his plan for us. We can know of a certainty in whom we have believed, that our Redeemer lives. Because he lives, we too shall live!

QUESTIONS FOR STUDY

1. If you have experienced the miracle of God's power to heal, tell about it. Was it in yourself? in another person? Was it physical healing or spiritual or both?

2. Discuss situations in which you tend to think and/ or speak negatively. How can you go about changing this?

3. Recall an incident when "faith-thinking" (positive thinking) changed a situation. Perhaps the situation remained the same, but the attitude about it became victorious not defeatist.

4. Have you ever prayed when you really did not expect your prayers to be answered? What thoughts do you have about this? How do you interpret the verse: "Lord I believe. Help thou my unbelief"?

5. If you have accepted a lesser potential of physical health, of mental achievement, or of spiritual victory because of lack of faith, what can you do about this? How does one start to make his faith work?

..{4}..

When Man Responds

Ted walked from the campus toward the river. He came
to a seldom-used railroad track, ignored the No Trespass-
ing sign, and made his way out onto a trestle.

Standing on a small, railed-in platform over the middle
of the river, he looked down at the dark waters swirling
below and thought about his aimlessly drifting life. Then
he looked up at the pinpoints of light spread across the
sky. Gazing at the constellations and sensing the certainty
of something far beyond only made Ted feel more out of
place in an orderly universe. Where, he asked himself,
had he first got off the track?

Ted had been reared in a religious home. When he was
ten years old his younger sister Gwen died of spinal men-
ingitis. This tragedy had a sobering effect on the boy. For
the next few years he went regularly to church and youth
meetings.

But during his last two years in high school, Ted's
prowess at football and basketball attracted attention and

43

brought him honors and adulation. Surrounded by the admiration of his friends, he became more and more the center of his own universe, careless about the need for a focal point beyond himself. God seemed an unnecessary inconvenience. Church was O.K. for his parents, but not for Ted.

At college he openly ran his own life, and there were plenty of opportunities to sample "forbidden fruit"— alcohol, drugs, sex. But indulgence took its toll. Ted's schoolwork suffered, and he lost his scholarship aid. His parents began to scold, and the gulf between them and their son grew wider.

His innate common sense made Ted determine to assert his will power, get back on the dean's list, and recover his scholarship. At the same time he knew how much he desired the approval of his peers, and the easy availability of instant physical pleasure held him in a firm grip. His loneliness of spirit remained. There was no gleam in his eyes, no real hope in his heart. He resisted the moral imperative, the "ought" which he knew he should obey.

One night Ted heard a member of the Peace Corps describe his two years in South America, his joy of serving even in the midst of disease, poverty, and frequent danger. He referred to the people among whom he had lived and worked as "my brothers," and something stirred deep within Ted's heart.

Now, standing on the railroad trestle and staring down into the dark waters below, he was acutely conscious of how pointless his life had become. He looked up at the stars and again something stirred within him. He thought about his sister Gwen, long dead. He recalled countless kindnesses his parents had performed—for instance, how

they had taken turns sitting up, night after night, with a
neighbor who had been gravely injured.

On an impulse, Ted reached into his pocket, pulled out
an envelope of pot, and threw it into the river. He knew
how much he had come to rely on outer stimulants, how
often he had sought forgetfulness in liquor and drugs.
He also recalled how often he had cheated in his schoolwork, how many lies he had told, how entrenched had become his habit of seeing others—especially girls—as means
to provide him with pleasure and approval. In his imagination, Ted slowly gathered all these together and deliber-
ately threw them one by one into the stream below.

Suddenly he felt stripped and helpless, and for a moment
he was seized by a terrifying loneliness. What could he do
now? Further lies and deception would not help. How
could he fill his emptiness? If he were really breaking with
the past, pot and pills would no longer be available to give
him a lift and let him escape life's problems. All his
crutches had been tossed into the river.

In his crisis of spirit, Ted lifted his eyes once more and
tried to see beyond the stars. "There must be a God," he
whispered to himself. "There *is* a God—Gwen's God, my
father's God, *my* God."

The void was filled. Into Ted's mind and soul came an
overpowering sense of the presence of God. Of course
. . . of course, it was all true. Life was *not* meaningless;
there *was* meaning and power. And all the peoples of the
earth . . . of course! They were his brothers. He could
—he would—go back to school and get to work. Not only
for his own sake, but for theirs. From that moment on, his
life had purpose.

Man has to come to a place of decision, for God will not

force a response. He will not burglarize his way into a man's life. He honors the freedom that he has given his children. Therefore, any response on man's part must come of his own free choice.

The choice is always ours. Jesus was alone in the Garden of Gethsemane in a struggle so agonizing that he sweat blood. When he came to a decision it was his very own. "Thy will be done," Jesus prayed, and immediately God flooded his heart with peace and power.

When we make our decisions for or against God, we stand alone. The choice is individual and personal. True, life becomes less meaningful to him who refuses God's love. The road becomes harder if he resists God's will for him. But whenever the decision is made in God's favor, the resources of his Spirit are ours and victory is assured. To be effective, however, the decisions must come from within a man's own heart.

A youth joins the church because his parents wish it; a man signs up as a church member to please his wife or to gain status in the community—such decisions are the result of outer pressure rather than inner conviction. They do not spring from a deep inner need, and consequently they will have to be made over again someday on the right basis or they will bring no lasting meaning or power to life.

Man's decision to discover and do God's will must be complete and unconditional if he is to know God's power in its abundance. A partial commitment curtails that divine power. What is more, to make one's commitment dependent on circumstances or on what others may do is to rob oneself of joyous abandon. The experience of the swimmer who gingerly eases himself into the pool, clinging fearfully to the ladder, in no way compares to that of the one who leaps from the diving board!

I once heard a youngster describe the leap of faith this way: "I've burned every bridge behind me. I've no place to retreat. Now, if God lets me down, I'm really sunk!"

This quality of dedication ensures a fullness of God's power. We give him our weakness; he gives us his strength. We give him our sin; he gives us his righteousness. He replaces our hatred with his love. In return for our fear, he gives us his confidence. As we give him our all, he gives us his all.

A man's response is always an act of faith. He goes out like Abraham, "not knowing where he is going" and "endures as seeing him who is invisible." If we could see into the future and know the results of our decisions, there would be no need for faith. To have faith is to play the hunches that come to us, to "trust the soul's invincible surmise," to act as if God is there and faith in him really will work. Wonder of wonders, we discover that God *is* there and faith *does* work!

Responding to God is something like being a scientist and staking your time and reputation on a great experiment. In a laboratory, researchers discover and then test the uniformity and trustworthiness of certain laws. This gives them an experience of dependability in one area of nature which they then try to apply to other areas. Experiences, whether scientific or spiritual, are not granted by magic or to a favored few. They come as the result of courageous, and often painstaking, experimentation.

Jesus did not begin his ministry to his disciples with the reassuring words, "Abide in me and I will abide in you," but with the command, "Follow me." He called his disciples to adventure and experimentation. As a result of their obedience, they found an experience of fellowship and friendship far beyond anything they could have imagined.

Donald Hankey once said, "Religion is betting your life on God." Today the church needs men with the will to believe that the way of Christ is the hope of the world. When men believe this and act out their faith, life takes on new meaning and the incidence of surprises increases greatly. Existence takes on a note of joy and a quality of hope that surpass anything in our previous experience.

The will to believe goes hand in hand with the willingness to venture. Often we find ourselves poised between fear and faith, action and inaction. The yearning to withdraw does battle with the desire to venture forth. God is calling us to walk in the footsteps of him who said, "He who loses his life shall find it." Paul speaks of "hazarding our lives for the gospel." It is one thing for a football team to see a play diagramed on the blackboard and believe that it will work; it is another thing to put the play into action on the field. Countless attempts, failures, reassessments, and a great deal of discipline go into the process. Shall it be any less so in the game of life? Here, too, there are failures, new lessons to be learned, new beginnings to be made, and the need for perseverance and total commitment.

Crowning the will to believe and to venture is the will to love. A life that lacks the spirit of love must ultimately fail. We may not command ourselves to love, but we can easily place ourselves in a position where love will begin to grow. For example, I can choose whether to harbor a grudge against someone or pray for him. I can choose whether to be bored by a conversation or listen attentively and get beyond the other person's words, feeling my way into his being. If I want to love and take appropriate steps, God will supply the love.

In the case where there is a barrier between myself and another, I may not be able to move immediately into an attitude of love. Nevertheless, there are certain steps that I can take.

(1) I can see him in terms of his needs and not his faults (for example, not his tardiness but his inability to plan, not his drinking but his loneliness, not his boisterousness but his insecurity).

(2) I can empathize with him. Pity is not love, but it is often a stepping stone to love. And far better than pity is identification with the other person's condition and circumstances. I can stop judging, even as Jesus commanded (Matt. 7:1).

(3) I can pray for him and see him as one of God's children. I can pray that God's strength and guidance may be his; I can pray to love him with the kind of love God has for him.

(4) I can do something for him—something concrete that meets his needs or desires.

In all this, it is good to remember that the response of Christians to the love of God is all too frequently in terms of *quantity* rather than *quality*. People are challenged by the gospel and respond by increasing their church pledges, doing more church work, taking on extra tasks at home or in the community. This could possibly be the direction in which God is calling, but taking on extra tasks could also be an escape from the necessity to capitulate at the inner core of our beings. *We prefer to work harder rather than to be different.*

God does not want our labor and gifts as much as he wants us. We may go through the outward motions that indicate discipleship, yet remain unyielded at the center —touchy, protective, reserving the right at last to run our own lives, to cherish our own moods, and to think or do as we please. God asks for a quality of dedication wherein the very "I" within each of us is yielded and given over to do his will.

The only thing we truly possess is the will to choose or refuse to do God's will. Jesus said, "If any man would be my disciple, let him deny himself." He did not say deny himself some pleasure, some habit, some money, or some leisure time, but deny *himself*. The inner citadel must be stormed and must surrender.

Why do we refer to this yielding of the inner self as a victory rather than a defeat? Because it takes place in response to the great love of God. The Heavenly Father has followed us, believed in us, forgiven us, showered us with countless gifts. His eternal love is given to us and for us, personified and made available in Jesus Christ.

Like the young man Ted, each of us stands by the river of life, faced with the necessity of making a choice and finding the direction we should take. We may cast into the stream all that has held us enslaved, all that has estranged us from our fellow-men and from our Heavenly Father. Then we may give ourselves entirely to him to be his obedient servants forever. Our theme song then becomes,

Love so amazing, so divine
Demands my soul, my life, my all.

Demands my all—yes; and now *has* it. We offer ourselves to become God's servants. However, he does not call us servants, but friends. He welcomes us as members of his family. "We are children of God, and if children, then heirs, heirs of God and fellow heirs with Christ" (Rom. 8:16–17, RSV).

QUESTIONS FOR STUDY

1. When there have been some times of aimlessness and drifting in your life, what helped you to find purpose? What part did fellowship, or the love of another, play in this change in attitude?

2. When was the first time you made a commitment of your life to Christ? Was this a specific occasion you can pinpoint? Was this final or do you feel the need of a new and deeper commitment from time to time? If you feel an urge to take a new step in spiritual growth, what would it entail?

3. Discuss the steps by which you have been able to love unlovely people. Think of one specific person: relative? in-law? neighbor? work partner?

4. Recall some instance of abandon and the giving of your total self to some project or game. Do you have this same kind of abandon in your commitment to Christ? How can you achieve this exciting adventure?

PART II

··{ 5 }··

Part of the Curse or Part of the Cure?

It was quite an honor for the college professor. An honor, yes, but one that carried with it a good deal of responsibility. He had been named by the president of the United States as one of a seven-member commission to arbitrate a border dispute between America and Mexico and recommend a settlement.

The commission had been at work for several months when one day the professor was struck by the ironic realization that in his private life he was carrying on his own border dispute. For ten years he had not exchanged a word with the neighbor who owned the property next to his summer home. This war of silence had begun when the professor carelessly planted some shrubs a few feet over the boundary line in the neighbor's land. The neighbor promptly dug them up, and the professor retaliated by building a fence between the two properties.

Now, after a decade of enmity, the professor's conscience began to trouble him. How hypocritical it was to seek a peaceful solution to an international boundary dispute when he had done nothing to settle the dispute that existed in his own backyard.

At the first opportunity, he went to his neighbor and apologized for his original carelessness and his subsequent stubbornness. The neighbor not only accepted his apology but acknowledged his own resentment in the matter. The next day the two men celebrated their restored friendship by working together to tear down the fence.

Jesus had a "magnificent obsession" to build the Kingdom of God. This Kingdom was not only a dream in his heart, but a plan for mankind that would endure till the end of time. It was reinforced by Jesus' personal life, which embodied its spirit and principles. He lived in a world of problems; however, he did not reflect these problems in himself but lived above and beyond them. "Be of good cheer," he said, "I have overcome the world." His life pointed the way and supplied solutions to the annoying situations that continually arose.

The world today is no less plagued with problems. It is easy to become discouraged and frustrated when we contemplate the multitude of disputes that surround us and make life difficult. But the Good News is that we need not be part of the curse; we can be part of the cure.

Not long ago I led a retreat for a group of young people who were vitally interested in world missions. They had raised money for this retreat by a variety of projects—among them, putting on plays and sponsoring car-washes. They had also been involved in a study group to learn more about the needs of the world.

As I faced those young people, I spoke of Jesus Christ

as the hope of the world and the answer to its needs. I opened my life, confessing that although I was a Christian I did not always live a quality of life that brought answers; in fact, I had often added to the world's problems.

"For instance," I said, "I once shared the leadership of a meeting with a fellow minister. At the close of the meeting, several people came up to him, thanking him for his helpfulness, but no one came to me. I was jealous, for in my heart I was fiercely competitive and determined to outshine him. Pride and the world's cutthroat spirit had found their way into my life. At that moment I was part of the curse, not the cure. It was only when I admitted my attitude and asked this man's forgiveness that I felt release from my guilt and was again free to become part of the cure for the world's ills."

The young people listened attentively, and in a few moments they were supplying feedback.

"I'm always walking over my younger sister," one girl admitted, "fighting and quarreling with her and putting her in her place. Then I come to church like an angel and sing in the choir."

Another girl broke in, "I know I should be more agreeable at home, but I just don't want to."

A young man, a junior in high school, added, "My English teacher is so crabby; she's been that way for years. But I never thought of looking at her as a person—a human being with feelings."

Another fellow said, "Sure, I like my parents, but I never tell them so. I guess they represent a roof over my head and food on the table. In fact, my home is not much more to me than a garage and a telephone booth. It never occurred to me that my parents are really concerned about me—that they are persons who might be lonely, who might need my friendship."

"I do my share of work around the house," interjected a young girl, "but I always let everyone know how much I hate it."

There were other, similar confessions, as these youths began to see how they were failing in their personal lives and as members of families. Then came time for prayer.

"God, forgive me for fighting with my sister. Help me to take an interest in her and see her point of view."

"Dear God, let me see my English teacher as you see her —a person with feelings who is doing her best. Help me to cooperate with her."

"Show me how to get closer to my parents."

"Dear Lord, give me a new attitude so I will enjoy doing things around the house. Help me to be grateful for all I have received."

Those earnest young people recognized that in commonplace ways they had been part of the divisiveness of the world, just as I had in my jealousy. They now determined to be part of its reconciliation. Rather than representing a generation gap, they wanted to be part of a communication link.

It is somewhat futile to talk about peace in the world if we cannot change the relationships in our own homes, at school, or on the job. But the sad fact is that we are more adept at responding with hostility than with love.

How we retaliate, returning threat for threat and blow for blow! An attack, real or fancied, on a destroyer in Tonkin Bay blows up into a full-scale war. This type of incident occurs constantly at every level of life because men react in anger and do not consider the consequences of retaliation.

Broken friendships, divorce, political feuds, and outright physical conflict all stem from our facility to respond negatively, from our touchiness and competitive spirit, from our desire to be "in the right." And if we are quick to hate, we are slow to forgive. From infancy on we seem to be schooled in the way of war rather than the way of peace. What a far cry all this is from the spirit of the Master, who lived among temperamental and quarrelsome disciples, returning good for evil, responding to fiery tempers with poised firmness and love, and offering forgiveness that knew no limits.

The world declares dogmatically, "Human nature cannot be changed." To which the Christian replies, "Oh, yes, it can!" Let me share with you a few stories of modern-day miracles—true stories of men and women who found that human nature can be changed.

A woman, married to an alcoholic husband with a violent temper, lived in constant fear that one day he would carry out his threats to kill her. But in Christ she found victory over the fear of death and returned to her home unafraid, ready to love her man and to minister to his needs, regardless of threats and abuse. Slowly but surely, love—selfless and undemanding—is winning him over.

A father ruled his family with an iron hand, seeing his children's smoldering rebellion but always squelching it. At a conference he was brought face to face with his authoritarianism, and he had the honesty to stand up and say in public, "I see that I have been trusting in force, not in fellowship. I have tried to instill fear instead of love. But I am going home to make friends with my family."

Easy? Of course not. But possible, with the resources of God's love and power.

A husband and wife had both agreed to a divorce as soon as the children had finished school. They continued to live in the same house, but stubbornness and disagreement kept them far apart. Anything was tinder for a new domestic explosion: the color of paint for the hallway; the make of car to buy; how to vote in the school-board election.

Somehow, perhaps under pressure from friends, they found their way to a couples' retreat, and there they saw living examples of God at work in the lives of people very much like them. They saw the folly of their wasted years; their hearts were melted; and when they became honest and open with each other, they felt married anew.

Another husband at that same retreat spoke of the way in which he had sought to manipulate his wife. He asked her forgiveness and prayed to God to help him set her free to be herself. Until that moment he had been contributing to the world's dictatorship. But now he joined forces with the fellowship that aims to set people free from manipulation for selfish ends.

All too clearly have I seen this pattern repeated in my own life. As a pastor I was an avid worker for missions, priding myself on raising more than the quota assigned to my church. Mission-study classes, missionary instruction in the church school, and mission-centered sermons were part of my standard operating procedure.

Yet I myself was in constant inner turmoil, harassed by fears and nervous breakdowns. How pathetic it was to be preaching peace for the world and not to know peace in my own heart! How easy to overlook the problems in my own backyard and dedicate myself to what was far away! Loving praise, I was willing to be elevated to a pedestal by admiring parishioners—to become their petty god. I could not bear for people to know that I was not the same man under my mask that I appeared to be on the surface.

The day finally came when my inner conflict was so intolerable that there seemed no other way to peace than to break through the veneer, remove the mask, and live in honesty and openness. Haltingly at first, I let myself be known to my fellow-men. There followed a release of tension and an experience of wholeness as I received the quiet assurance that my Heavenly Father loved me regardless of my mistakes and shortcomings. My ministry was no longer a frantic effort to cover up inner discord while working for harmony among others. The newly found peace in my own life had become a part of God's peace in the world. The missionary program in which I labored now became the extension and the fulfillment of that which God had already planted in my heart.

So it is that we are either part of the world's stalemate —a peace conference held up by the shape of a table, a couple stymied by disagreement over what kind of car to buy—or a part of the reconciling force in which selfish wills are yielded to God's will. In this reconciling force, men and women discover peace, healing, and a common purpose for their lives.

Contributing to answers for the world, rather than adding to its problems, is not so much a way of acting as it is the overflow of a way of being. The incarnation did not mean merely that Jesus acted in a godly way. It meant that God lived in and through him. God lived his life of constant love through Jesus because Jesus was fully yielded to his father.

The Good News is that God would do the same in us! He desires that Christ be formed in us (Gal. 4:19); that we become new creatures in Christ Jesus (2 Cor. 5:17); and that what we do is because the Father who dwells in us does his work through us (John 14:10).

God through Christ would live in us in such a way that we are not perpetually straining to do the things which contribute to the world's well-being. It is more a matter of our simply living out in the world the answer that God has already given to us in Christ. At its best, this style of life is virtually effortless and unconscious. It is just *being* —being exciting new creatures in Christ.

QUESTIONS FOR STUDY

1. Are there some phases of your life where you are contributing to the solution of the world's ills rather than adding to its problems? How did you learn to have this kind of concern?

2. Are there places in your life where you may be adding to the world's problems? What can God help you to do about these?

3. Are you more adept at peace-making than barrier-building? Are your points of view more important to you than the building of friendships?

4. Some of the secrets of getting closer to people are identifying with their interests, listening, etc. Mention others. In which are you strong? Which do you need to cultivate? How will you go about it?

··{ 6 }··

Discovering God's Plan

God's plan for his creation embraces everything, from the movement of the remotest star to the unfolding of the tiniest flower. And he has a plan for every human life. Each of us is free to seek out God's plan and free also to accept or reject it. When a man chooses God's plan, he reaches his highest potential, finds and fulfills the destiny for which he was born.

God accepts the primary responsibility for making his plans known to us. An earthly parent is anxious to communicate his wishes to his offspring; how much more eager is the Heavenly Father to make his will known to his children. Therefore the emphasis in our lives should not be so much trying to ascertain the will of God as seeking fellowship with the Father so that he may communicate his will to us.

I believe our spiritual approach is wrong if we forever beseech God for answers to our questions, solutions to our problems, directions in times of perplexity. Rather, we should seek him for *himself*. It is heartache for a parent if his child only comes to him in times of trouble, and then only that he might be extricated from it. In such a relationship there is scant fellowship, little building of a warm comradeship. Just so there is pain in the heart of God when we neglect him except when we need to be rescued from difficulties. At such times he may well hide himself from us in order that we may, in our extremity, seek him for himself.

There was a time in my life when I was seeking a new pastorate, and I prayed very earnestly that God would open the door to another church and show me where to go. I was quite perplexed that no church sought me out and no door seemed to open. Why did God not answer my prayers?

In my perplexity I threw myself on God and asked him to show me the reason for these months of delay. As I quietly searched my heart, he showed me that I was more interested in a promotion, a larger salary, and a more influential church than I was in really seeking his will. In my pride and egotism, I wanted God's will, all right, but on my own terms!

When my sin was clear to me, I sought God as my forgiving Father and experienced an overwhelming sense of his love and presence. What a change in my attitude! Now I came to God in a spirit of reconciliation and fellowship. My immediate problem—finding a new job— was temporarily laid aside. Without realizing it, I found myself saying, "God, I'll go anywhere you want me to go."

Within a few days the door opened to a pastorate that at first seemed very unattractive, but which proved to be the field of fifteen years of joyous, fruitful work. The problem was solved when I was willing to come to God not for the solution to a problem but for forgiveness and the reestablishment of a relationship.

When we seek God for himself, he makes good his desire to communicate with us. It then becomes our responsibility to listen to him. "When man listens, God speaks."

The prerequisite for listening to God and discerning his will is a sincere desire to be obedient to that will. Paul writes, "Let your minds be remade and your whole nature thus transformed. Then [not before!] will you be able to discern the will of God" (Rom. 12:2, NEB). Knowing the will of God, therefore, depends on our willingness to be yielded to him.

I have found four attitudes to be of great value in discovering and doing the will of God. They are *acceptance, relinquishment, freedom,* and *obedience.*

Acceptance. Most people feel pressured by life, hemmed in by circumstances, harried by fears and anxieties, or threatened by the opinions of others. In such a framework we can only *react* to life. Instead of acting in harmony with God's will, we are at the mercy of circumstances, reacting within a mood of fear, pressure, or bitterness, allowing negative forces to dictate our decisions. This is a far cry from Paul's words, "Let Christ's peace be arbiter in your hearts" (Col. 3:15, NEB).

The attitude of acceptance provides a way out of this slavery to circumstances. While it is true that if acceptance were the only attitude available to us we would be little more than "doormats," nevertheless as one of four principles it is an important factor in placing us in the frame of mind wherein we may more readily recognize God's will.

To determine the degree of acceptance in your own life, ask yourself the following questions:

Have I accepted myself and my life situation? Can I look in the mirror and say, "I thank God that I'm me"? Have I accepted my age, my state of health, my limitations, my education, and given thanks to God for what is? Have I accepted my financial status, my place in society, my heredity?

When we stop living in "if-only" land, longing for different circumstances, and learn to thank God for our lives as they are, we are at the gateway to victorious living. Then we can really praise and thank God for present situations.

After such a soul-searching, you may become aware of many places in your life where you have been discontent or even rebellious. On reflection you may recall areas of unforgiven sin in your life, or mistakes that have not been faced honestly and for which restitution has not been made. Look at them squarely, turn them over to God, ask his forgiveness, and promise to do whatever he wishes you to do about them.

Face also the things that bug you and curtail your effectiveness—fear of failure, fear of making mistakes, fear of what other people may think or say, fear of being laughed at. Will you, right now, quietly but wholeheartedly, face the totality of life—yourself, your situation, your past and future, the people among whom you live and work? Will you tell God that even if these circumstances and people remain unchanged for the rest of your

life you will accept yourself and your situation as it is and
thank God for it?

Relinquishment. This second attitude involves the placing of one's total life situation into the hands of God.
Merely to accept life would be stoicism, bowing our necks
to the bludgeonings of life in brave submission. But the
Christian places all the circumstances of his life in the
hands of God, knowing that God is ever at work in and
through them for good (Rom. 8:28).

This act of relinquishment lifts the burden from our
shoulders and places it on God, as he has invited us to do.
In 1 Peter we find the injunction, "Cast all your anxieties
on him, for he cares about you" (1 Pet. 5:7, rsv). The
load and the responsibility are now his.

There is a simple mechanical device that may help you
take this step. Write down on a sheet of paper all the
things that trouble you and cause fear and anxiety. Oppo-
site these, or under them, make a list of all the things for
which you are grateful. Then, in prayer, tell God that
you accept your life situation in its totality. Accept each
situation, one by one. Tell God that you are willing not
only to face it, but to seek to know what God is trying to
say to you through that particular circumstance. Thank
God for the good things. Then burn the paper as symbolic evidence that you have placed your entire life in his
hands with no time limit and without reservations.

Or you may use the cupped hands device described at
the beginning of chapter 3. Filling the hands with life's
anxieties and problems is a symbolic act of acceptance;
turning them over to let the contents run out is a sign of
relinquishment. The second upturning of the hands then

becomes a symbol of receiving God's forgiveness and empowering presence.

There is always a tendency to take back what we have given to God. Our emotions and reflexes frequently re-assert themselves. Therefore these acts of acceptance and relinquishment need to be repeated. We must leave in his hands what we have freely given to him, remembering that the burden rests on him and not on us. This may be a daily, sometimes an hourly, necessity.

Freedom. Acceptance and relinquishment prepare the way for the embracing of freedom. Having accepted whatever people may think, we are freed from the fear of their opinions. What they may say is no longer the cri-terion; what God says is what counts. We can listen to people, evaluate their words, give them over to God, and let him speak his wisdom to us.

We are set free also from the fear of failure. Neither failure nor success can hamper us because these have been placed in God's hands.

Suppose for a moment that a superintendent of schools hired a certain young man as a teacher in the adult educa-tion department. For two years this young man taught. His classes were marked by quarreling and jealousy, and every member of the class failed the final exam. Would you call this young man a successful teacher? Yet this describes the record of Jesus, for all of his disciples fled and deserted him on that final night.

Jesus was an *apparent* failure, but history has proved him to be the most effective leader of all time. The Christ-ian is not called to be successful, but to be faithful. He is set free from the fear of failure or the compulsion to suc-ceed. God can use his mistakes and turn his apparent failures into the means of advancing his Kingdom, even as he turned Calvary into Easter.

A pitcher that is already full cannot be further filled. A life that is crowded with worry has no room for the peace and assurance of God. But when the pitcher is emptied, it is ready to receive new contents. In just the same way, when the pitcher of our life is emptied of old fears and anxieties, God fills the vacant place with his presence. A spirit of thanksgiving pervades our hearts. It is impossible to worry and give thanks at the same time, for these two attitudes are mutually exclusive.

God has not only set us free *from*, but free *for*. Now that the fears of people and of failure have been taken away, we are free to be ourselves. Some psychologists say that most of us use only 10 to 20 percent of our potential. We are created in God's image, with an enormous capacity for loyalty and caring. Our God, whose life is one of "steadfast loyalty," has given this spirit to us also.

The human spirit is made to care and to love. The entire universe operates on the principle of cooperation and unity, but the only way this will ultimately work among men and among nations is when the way of Jesus Christ, which is the love of God, is lived out in daily lives.

We have often heard it said that the human spirit is basically selfish. I do not believe this to be true. Not self-preservation, but the preservation of the species is the first law of nature. Otherwise, there would be no self to preserve! This instinct is altruistic and motivated by love. In times of great tragedies and catastrophes, man's deep caring is called to the fore.

God sets us free to be our real selves, that is, to create, to dream, to love, to care, to listen, to be a friend to our fellows. He sets us free from the early training that has inhibited or warped us. He gives us the power to break through self-consciousness and the fear of rejection. We are free to love and care with an imaginative awareness of the needs of others.

We are set free also to use the talents God has given us. In the parable of the talents, the man who had only one was afraid, and buried his capacities (Matt. 25:25). God sets us free from this kind of fear, free to use our inner potential with ever-increasing confidence. We are free indeed when we are free to fulfill the blueprint that God has drawn for our lives.

Obedience. The fourth step in this "new path of life" (Rom. 6:4, NEB) is our willingness to be quickly and joyously obedient. The life that is set free abounds with hunches, with possible courses of action, ideas, and plans. We have a new awareness of the person we can become, of helpful things we may do, of persons we may befriend, of truths we may speak. Above all, we have a new spirit with which we may approach routine daily tasks. There is a new joy as we meet "the same old people" every day at home or on the job.

When these impulses or hunches come, let us test them to see if they harmonize with the Spirit of Jesus and, if so, act on them at once. To be most effective, obedience should be immediate. A nimble, responsive spirit is quickly at God's disposal and is powerful in its contribution to the Kingdom.

Obedience to the will of God may bring us to take action on some things that we have previously neglected or "accepted." For example, it may lead us to ask for a raise in pay, or to fight for a cleaner city, or to protest against injustice, or to look for another job, or to pray for the healing of some bodily ailment. But whatever we do, we will not be reacting angrily or impatiently against our life situations, for we have already accepted them. Rather, we will be moving out in obedience to God's leading, motivated by his love. We never get the feeling that Jesus reacted to people, but rather that he spoke and acted out of his great concern for them, with a never-ending supply of love from the heart of God.

Obedience deepens our knowledge of God's will and sets the stage for him to show us further plans that he has for us. As we are faithful in little, we shall have the opportunity to be faithful in much.

However, we cannot take God's leadings "on approval," the way a woman may buy a hat, not sure whether she wants to keep it or return it to the store. There must be a willingness to accept the will of God whatever it may be, otherwise our understanding of his will is warped by our selfish desires. Once we are willing to be and to do whatever he wants, then God can get through to us, for we are listening without reservations.

The phrase *the will of God* often has a somber and dampening impact on people. It can suggest the kind of resignation and submission that crushes all human initiative.

More than half a century ago I conducted the funeral of a little girl who had died of diphtheria. Her family lived in an unsanitary section of the village, "on the wrong side of the tracks." Some of the church people who lived in nice homes with running water and modern sewage systems were heard to say, "What a shame she had to die, but we must accept God's will."

Such an attitude is blasphemy. That little girl's death was not God's will. It was God's will that unsanitary conditions in that village be changed and children's health protected so that they could grow to Christian adulthood!

Instead of seeing God's will as something that demands submission, see it as if you are a soldier, saluting a captain, and responding to his command. The great Captain moves on to build his Kingdom and calls us to follow. Our response is, "Yes, Master. Your will shall be done."

It is often at the growing edge of our lives that we discover God's will, and it may require taking only a single step. A man once said to me, "God mercifully did not reveal all my sins to me at once. If he had, I would have given up then and there." The step that God reveals may be a simple one or it may be very dramatic and completely different from anything we have done before. Paul's next step on the Damascus Road was to go to the city, find Ananias, and ascertain further the will of God. Someone's next step may be simply to write a letter, to make restitution, to apologize, or to begin building a bridge of friendship to someone else.

If a person wants to unravel a ball of twine that is all snarled, he turns the ball over and over until he finds a loose end. Beginning at that point, he unravels the entire ball step by step. The Chinese proverb expresses it, "The longest journey starts with a single step." God is very much a realist, asking us to begin in the present situation. There is nothing wrong with the desire to right the world's wrongs, correct injustices of a monumental nature, and transform evil institutions. But to get lost in dreams so large in scope may prevent us from seeing that God is asking us to meet an immediate situation and to take a simple, though difficult, next step in the here and now.

At first glance, the next step may seem trivial indeed. For young Kate Lawrence it was to do household chores without whining. For Jerry Groves, a high-school student, it was to see his teachers as human beings with feelings and not as enemies to be plagued and bullied. For Sam Morris it was to offer to share a piece of cake at lunchtime with a man in his shop, although they had not spoken a civil word to each other in years. These were all small steps, yet all were followed by radical, far-reaching results.

People often ask, "How can I know the will of God?"

This is, of course, no simple question. But the New Testament helps us here, for in it the emphasis is never on *knowing* but always on *doing*. In the Lord's Prayer, it is "Thy will be done," not "Thy will be known." In the Garden of Gethsemane, Jesus did not ask to know the will of God, but offered himself to do that will.

On another occasion, Jesus said, "If any man's will is to do his will, he shall know whether the teaching is from God" (John 7:17, RSV). Here knowledge follows obedience. If we know in advance, with certainty, what the will of God is in every detail, there is little room for faith. Faith often requires putting our hand into the hand of God, walking into the darkness, going out like Abraham "not knowing where he was to go" (Heb. 11:8, RSV). The important question is not, "How do I *know* the will of God?" but, "Am I willing to *do* the will of God?"

His will may become evident as we check on our attitudes. A young couple came to my home, concerned that they were not doing enough for the Kingdom. They never could seem to find "the right church" or "the right places to work" or "the right people" to whom to witness. As we talked, it became evident that the two felt barriers between themselves. Critical attitudes had developed in the home as well as on the job. When these were laid bare and restitution made, there was an immediate sense of peace and an inner assurance that God's direction would be given to them. Too often we blame circumstances when the place to look for the difficulty is within ourselves.

God's will for us also comes in the form of hunches to be acted upon. These hunches are variously named leadings, impulses, intuition, guidance, promptings of the Spirit, and the like. For most people, these leadings come as coherent thoughts. A few people have visual images and see what God would have them do. Others hear a voice speaking clearly. But the vast majority simply "get an idea" or "feel a pull" or "have a hunch."

Playing these hunches and following these impulses may involve risk. Most church folks are conservative, slow to abandon old pathways and venture into new ones. But Jesus said, "They of old said . . . but I say to you . . ." He pioneered, and he asks that we follow him into new adventures. To follow Christ means to risk failure. Roger Shinn reminds us that we need to rely on God's forgiveness rather than on our certainties. It is by making mistakes that we learn. When we blunder, God's Spirit, the inner voice, corrects us and brings us back on target if we are teachable and willing to listen. God cannot use zero, but he can and does use our blunders. Sometimes it seems that he has little else to use but mistakes! What mighty things he does through very unworthy and faulty means!

Obedience leads to maturity, for it is by obeying that we gain insight into the will of God. Through obedience we become more sensitive to his will, while constant disobedience blinds us to it. We may know for a long period of time what is the will of God in a particular instance, yet circumvent it, leave it undone, and try to go ahead while ignoring it.

In my own life, I knew for seventeen years that I should be really honest with my wife, but I dreaded this so much that I put it off month after month, year after year. When I finally crashed through, my whole life and ministry took on an entirely new dimension. To refuse to do what we know to be right limits our potential and keeps us from further ascertaining God's will.

When Mary and Joseph lost Jesus, they had to go back to the temple, the place where they had lost him. When you and I find that we have lost the power of God, we have to go back to the place where we disobeyed him. This done, we are in power once again.

QUESTIONS FOR STUDY

1. Are there people or situations that "get your goat"? What is it in you that is threatened in these instances? What are your areas of sensitivity (the places where you are touchy)—health? grooming? intelligence? economic status? others?

2. As a group, go through the action of the cupped hands (described in chap. 3), filling them and turning them over (Acceptance and Relinquishment) and then the final turning them up to receive God and his gifts. Let this be done without haste. Share with each other what happened.

3. Discuss the eagerness and immediacy, or the slowness and inertia, with which you obey God. How can your attitude be changed? How much of your reaction is a matter of temperament? How much a matter of unwillingness?

4. To be a Christian is to be free. Where do you feel free and where bound and unfree? What steps do you need to take to be free to fail, free from the fear of people's opinions, free to be yourself?

5. What difference is there between knowing and doing the will of God? Cite an example of doing the will of God when it meant moving out in a new direction. What emotional difficulties did you encounter as you made this decision?

6. Discuss hunches, feelings, leadings in thought-life (flash thoughts), happenings, sensing need in others, etc. Tell of experiences you have had along these lines.

··{7}··
Enjoy the Journey

Within recent years the ecological crisis in our country has become obvious. The issue is clear: either we clean up the atmosphere and live, or continue to pollute it and die.

The atmosphere in which we live is all-important to our physical and emotional well-being. If the air is full of smog, heavy with humidity and pollutants, we are apt to feel beaten and lifeless. Clean, crisp air and life-giving sunshine not only stimulate good health but also lift our spirits.

The spiritual air we breathe is equally important. We can live in an atmosphere of complaints, fault-finding, moodiness, and despair, and eventually destroy our inner well-being. Or we can live in an atmosphere of thanksgiving, praise, and an awareness of the workings of God in the world around us and enhance our spiritual vitality.

To change the kind of atmosphere in which we live, whether physical or spiritual, is a difficult assignment. But if we mean business, it can be done. If not, it spells death to body and soul.

The moment we awaken in the morning we can determine the mood of the day, just as a sailor sets his sails and, regardless of the wind direction, establishes the course which his ship will take. We can start the day problem-centered or resource-centered. In the first case, we think of all the difficult things we have to do. In the second, we think of the strength available to us from our Heavenly Father who will do his work through us and be our source of power all through the day.

There is a great difference between getting up with the despairing cry, "Good Lord! Morning!" and getting up with a joyous "Good morning, Lord!" And we may add, "This is the day the Lord has made; we will rejoice and be glad in it."

When I was a youngster, railroading was in its heyday. Huge coal-burning locomotives turned tons of water into live steam as they roared across the countryside. Tank towns were spaced out along the tracks. The locomotive would come to a stop beside one of these giant water reservoirs and the fireman would pull a huge pipe down into place. Water rushed from tank to tender, and the locomotive chugged off with a new supply.

Some trains, however, ran nonstop for long distances, and the amount of water that could be stored on board was insufficient for these long stretches. Engineers therefore built elongated shallow troughs along level stretches of track and filled the troughs with water. As the locomotive sped by, it let down a metal scoop into the trough, and the speed of the train forced the water up the scoop and connecting pipe into the engine or tender. In this way the locomotive was replenished while in motion.

In the spiritual life of a human being, there is a definite place for tank towns—worship services, conferences, special meetings, retreats. But wise is that man who has learned the art of being refilled while in action. It is possible to "sit loose" and live joyously so that a task leaves a man more refreshed than when he began.

The human heart itself has no tank towns. It never takes time out for rest, yet it keeps on working for years and years. The tiny pause between each heartbeat is the pause that refreshes and makes for continuous action.

A mother found herself tugging impatiently at her ten-year-old daughter's snarled hair. The school bus was due and the hair was a mess. Late rising had thrown the household into daily confusion. As on other mornings, while the mother yanked and scolded, trying to make Beth's hair presentable, the daughter gave way to tears of pain and anger.

After Beth had left the house, her mother sat down exhausted and deeply ashamed of her ill temper. That evening she asked the girl's forgiveness, and the two made a pact to get up earlier. The following morning there was ample time for the hair combing. And as the days passed, this morning task became a delightful ritual as mother and daughter chatted together and entered into a close fellowship. When Beth left for school, the mother went to her housework refreshed and with a song of gratitude in her heart.

A man's mood is often determined by his motives. If he strives for perfection in every act, he is apt to be tense and self-conscious, intent on never making a mistake. He lives in a state of perpetual self-reference. This prevents him from knowing the relaxed joy of one who flings himself into the game of life. A football player, heedless of personal injury, gives all his strength and attention to each play, knowing that losing and winning are both part of the game. He neither plays well nor enjoys the game if he concentrates on avoiding mistakes. The desire for perfection robs life of its joy, for fulfillment always remains just out of reach.

Have you found in your life that the desire to be good, the determination to achieve perfection, or the sense of doing your duty has diminished your joy and spontaneity and increased your fear of making mistakes? It is all too easy to direct one's religion mainly toward improving oneself, and less and less toward loving and enjoying one's fellow-men. The deeper joy comes not from pursuing personal goodness, but from willingly laying down one's life for the sake of others.

Sometimes when my wife and I would start out on a journey, she would look at me and ask, "Are you in a holiday mood?" And I would realize that I was gripping the steering wheel with grim determination, concentrating so hard on getting to my destination that I could enjoy neither the scenery along the road nor the companionship of my wife. The ride was a means to an end, not a pleasure in and of itself.

"The world is too much with us" so that we miss "heaven's music." Not only that, but the effort to live up to Christian ideals and accomplish church and community tasks produces a busyness that robs us of the day-by-day enjoyment of living, and takes away our appreciation of the people with whom we work. How sad to work hard to build God's Kingdom but not to have the spirit of the Kingdom in us while we work!

In our busyness we often assume that the harder we work the more quickly God's Kingdom will come. But the new day does not dawn for us or for society by dint of our prodigious efforts. It comes from doing, moment by moment, the will of God. This can be far more difficult than physical toil, as Jesus demonstrated in the garden. Gethsemane is not remembered for the amount of work that Jesus did, but for his struggle and eventual willingness to do God's will.

When we think about Jesus, we have the feeling that he "sat loose" and lived life deeply, with a leisurely fullness. He was constantly aware and appreciative of his Father's miracles in nature, calling attention to the lilies of the field and the birds of the air. He lived close to the joys and the heartaches of the world, without pressure or haste, with his eyes open to all that was going on around him. For Jesus, life was meant to be lived to the full.

We note that Paul could sing hymns at midnight in prison, for to him a cell was not a place to complain about, but rather a place where he could reach out to meet the needs of others. He worked through his own anxieties by ministering to the jailer—finding the answer to his own needs in serving someone else.

If you choose to ride in someone else's car, you must trust his driving. You cannot enjoy the trip if you are wishing all the while that he would drive differently. To be a good passenger—to relax and enjoy the ride—you must set him free to drive as he will.

How much more important to do this in the art of

living! If we constantly pressure people, worry them, wish they were different, and remain apprehensive about their next moves, life cannot be much fun for us, or for them either. Set people free; appreciate them as they are; and enjoy the journey as you travel down life's highway together.

Human beings—even those of us who are Christians and should know the meaning of true freedom—are too prone to live in the past or to fret about the future. To focus either on mistakes of the past or hazards of the future is to miss the richness of a life lived fully in the present. We can long for the good old days or mourn past failures, thus denying ourselves the joy and potential of the here and now. We can live in "if-only" land—the land that never seems to come—and thus fail to take advantage of and enjoyment in the moment at hand.

Deep faith in our Heavenly Father makes it possible for us to leave the past in his hands. We have sprung from the eternal heart of God, for we are created in his image. The mistakes and sins of our past have been caught up in his love. We may have "meant them for evil, but he has meant them for good" (see Gen. 50:20).

We stand in the present, grateful for the rich heritage and lessons of the past, and move confidently toward the future which God holds securely in his hands. We may not know *where* we are going, but we know *with whom* we are journeying. Thus we are set free to live fully in the now. Let us thank God for all that has been, for the miracle of what is, and for the haunting call of what is yet to be.

When I was a young boy, my parents frequently said to me, "If there's a wrong way to do a thing, you'll find it." The dread of making mistakes that grew within me robbed me of that carefree joy that we so often associate with childhood. As I grew older, I transferred this attitude of mind to my relationship with my Heavenly Father. I pictured God as a big policeman with an account book, eagerly noting all my misdeeds. I lived under the terror of doing wrong. Even my occasional periods of happy activity were punctuated by the dire thought that I might make a mistake at any moment. Not until years later did I realize that God wanted to liberate me from this binding memory of childhood, this fear of making mistakes, and free me to live with spontaneity and gladness, accepting mistake-making as part of life's normal learning process. Now, in the place of those words of childhood, I find myself saying, "Since there is a right way to do a thing, I know God will lead me to it."

As we may miss the joy of life by dwelling on the past, so we miss the possibilities of the present if we expect life's best days to be in the future. The good days are *now*. Here and now is where God is at work. Here and now is where God is asking us to work with him. The future should not hang over us like a cloud, making us live in dread of its uncertainty; neither should it beckon us with rosy promises that diminish the reality and importance of the present. The best preparation we can make for the future is to do God's will in the present.

What we choose to dwell on determines the emotional climate of our lives. A recently bereaved widow once said to me, "For a few weeks I gave way to grief. But one day God told me that my grief was basically caused by thinking about myself. It was a form of self-pity. I determined to start thanking God for my husband, recalling the many happy times we had together. I found that self-pity and thanksgiving were mutually exclusive."

The period of grief had served its purpose. To persist in it for an unreasonable length of time would have been to deny God's leading toward a victorious way of living.

As a pastor I denied myself much joy for many years by dwelling on the number of empty pews at a church service instead of thanking God for the people who were present. Frequent post-mortems following services robbed me of much happiness. Now I am learning a better way. I thank God for the people present, whether few or many, and at the close of the service I give the message over to God, thanking him for the privilege of being his messenger. I seldom deal with "feedback" until the following day or later.

This selective process also determines the attitude with which we approach our daily tasks. In the parable of the prodigal son, the elder brother says to his father, "You know how I have slaved for you all these years" (Luke 15:29, NEB). Like the rich young ruler, he had obeyed all the Father's commandments but had not found the key to life. He lived dutifully at home with his father, working hard, but feeling more like a slave than like a son!

We can let our jobs, our daily commuting, the tasks we do for the church, our school studies, and our household chores become a series of duties that enslave us and fill us with inner resentment and even rebellion.

In the parable the father tells his son, "All that I have is yours." But the son has become so bound by his duties on the farm that he has lost the spirit of forgiveness. The sound of music turns him off; an erring brother's return is cause for anger rather than rejoicing. Working, saving money, paying attention to daily tasks have pinched his spirit to the extent that he has never even given a party for his friends. He has truly become a slave. Everything on the estate is his to enjoy, yet he cannot enjoy it. What profit is it to gain the whole world and see the joy of life take flight?

God speaks to every one of his children when he says, "All that I have is yours." His gifts are spread out before us like food at a smorgasbord. We walk past his table and he bids us take what we will. His gifts are love, joy, peace, and countless other blessings. How strange that we often pass by his table and pick up some discarded scraps from a trash barrel. We choose "goodness" rather than joy, "conscientiousness" rather than freedom, "religion" rather than life! And our choices bring us nothing but rigidity and crippling paralysis, when we might have the freedom and laughter of that Man of Galilee who came that our joy might be full. The choice is always ours.

QUESTIONS FOR STUDY

1. Moodiness can be a real problem. If this is true in your case, do you want to be mastered by your moods, or to master them? What is God asking you to do about this?

2. Do you sometimes come to the end of the day exhausted, frustrated, or, on the other hand, relaxedly tired, with genuine joy? What produced these varied results?

3. Do you usually enjoy the people with whom you live and/or work? the tasks you perform? If so, what is your secret? If not, what is Christ asking you to do about it?

4. Recall the last occasion you were in a holiday mood. How can this mood be more prevalent?

5. What gifts will you take today from "God's smorgasbord"?

6. Try this experiment. As you awaken, still relaxed and sleepy, give the new day to God. As you retire for the night just as you are dropping off to sleep, give over to God's love the day just ended—its victories, its defeats; its joy, its sorrows. Murmur a heartfelt "Thank you, Father" as you slip into sleep. Your subconscious mind will take over. Then you will truly enjoy the journey!

··{ 8 }··

The Pathway to God

My first significant experience of a warm and vital fellowship with God began when I became willing to face up to the moral standards Jesus taught in the Sermon on the Mount. The real barrier to my fellowship with God was neither doctrinal nor religious. My failure was in the area of ethical behavior.

I needed to take a moral inventory of my life in the light of the teachings and life of Jesus. When I placed my life alongside that of the Master and sought to be drastically honest, I saw much that needed to be changed in myself. I had been a thief, padding expense accounts as treasurer of a ministerial association, no less! I had dishonestly allowed people to think that borrowed, brilliant sermon illustrations were my own. Yes, there was much deception and dishonesty in me.

As far as my sex life was concerned, outwardly I was without blemish. But periodically I gave way to lustful fantasies and reveled in sensuous reading.

I also recognized large areas of resentment and hostility —against certain fellow ministers, certain denominations, and various officials who opposed my way of running the church. Of course, I was too polite to admit this, and too skilled in deception to reveal it.

At home I was a dictator. Discipline and good behavior were much more important to me than a genuine outgoing love which would have allowed me to have happy, relaxed times with my family.

Added to all this was my persistent unwillingness to own up to any of these faults, either to my wife or my friends and associates.

When I saw the many places where I had fallen short of the standards of Jesus Christ, I began to make restitution by word and deed. I talked over my past with my wife and with a man who was a close friend. I spoke of all these hidden failures. Immediately there came an amazing emotional breakthrough. I felt that the real me was known by my wife and my friend. Both of them, aware of this inner part of me for the first time, were able to love me as I was, so that this real me felt loved as never before.

There is an old folk saying, "A friend is one who knows all about you, and loves you just the same." That was my experience—being deeply loved when I dropped my mask and revealed myself. Not only that, but there was an inrush of the joy and love of God that made me feel the presence of his Spirit in a way I had never known before. Willingness to face up to the ethical shortcomings in my life proved a prelude to crossing over the threshold into the presence and the fellowship of God.

There was much further growth that this increase in fellowship would demand, but the beginning was made when I took a moral inventory, became willing to be honest, and allowed my pride to be broken and laid low. There are still countless times when God asks me to be more transparent with my fellow-men. There will always be more moral rungs on the ladder for me to climb.

For many people, the breakthrough to God comes when they make the breakthrough to their fellow-men. John writes very explicitly: "He who does not love his brother whom he has seen, cannot love God whom he has not seen" (1 John 4:20, RSV). Barriers against our fellow-men are barriers against God. Jesus said that as we give love to one of the least of these his brethren, we do it unto him; when we withhold love, we withhold it from him (see Matt. 25:40, 45).

Not long ago I met with nine people from a certain parish where there was serious division. Having sensed dissatisfaction among his members, the pastor was contemplating leaving the church. In an atmosphere of Christian love we sought to discover God's plan for that man and for that congregation. First we asked the question, "What personal resentment or barrier is there for each one of us to consider, and what is God asking us to do about it?" In effect, each person was asking himself, "How can God change me?"

Within a few minutes, an eighteen-year-old young man was telling the pastor, "I don't feel close to you. I'm sorry; I wish I did. I liked the two previous pastors."

A deacon spoke up, "I have not always been sympathetic about your plans. And I have been disloyal, listening to unkind remarks about you, and sometimes adding a few of my own. Forgive me."

The pastor admitted, "I guess I'm stand-offish. I don't

mean to be unfriendly. But it's true—I like to have my own way, and I try to push through my plans rather than discovering the wishes of the group."

Every one of the nine had an apology to make and restitution to attempt. Tears and forgiveness flowed freely. After all had prayed, someone said, "Wouldn't it be great if the whole church were like this!"

Another replied, "This *is* the church, right here. Now we are the Body of Christ."

The church meeting where the pastor might have been asked to resign has come and gone, and the congregation is slowly but surely moving to a closer realization of the presence of God. The same doors that open to the love of man always open to the love of God.

Another pastor recently told me of a growing barren-ness in his life—the "fires of the Spirit" had burned very low. When I asked him to tell me about his church, he described a group of grumblers who were making things hard for him.

"Your very use of the word *grumblers*," I said, "locks people into that category and diminishes them. By using that word you are trying to establish your rightness and their wrongness. Will you stop using that term, and try to see your parishioners as God sees and loves them? Will you silently ask God what he wants you to do about building bridges of love to them?"

Within a few minutes there was a new light in the pastor's eyes. "I've been wrong to call them grumblers," he acknowledged. "I've often acted secretively and with-out their knowledge, and I owe some of them apologies and explanations."

As he grasped my hand I could see the light of God in his face.

Fellowship with God appears to be a variable thing for it is determined both by our trust and our obedience to him. We may stand proudly in church, singing hymns of adoration and affirming God's place of authority as we recite the Creed, and then in daily life do something quite different.

For example, to what extent are we dependent on money? Does a financial reverse upset us? Does a low salary cause continual annoyance and fretting? Are we more eager in the morning to read the Good News of the Bible or the latest stock market quotations? Do we fear financial insecurity? In other words, is God or gold more important to us? Jesus said, "You cannot serve God and Money" (Matt. 6:24, NEB).

We can learn a lot about what we truly depend on by asking ourselves, "To what do I turn in times of fatigue?" Physical rest? A drink? The television set? More work?

I remember once being spent and empty after several days on the road. I stood at an airport newsstand and looked over the paperback books. Something in me wanted to pamper my fatigue with some mild erotica. Despite what I may sing about or say in church, what I turn to in times of emptiness is really my god at the moment! And it may not be an obvious escape mechanism; it can as easily be ill temper or self-pity!

Times of fatigue afford a marvelous opportunity to let God reach down into the depths of our being. In weariness, our guard is down and the negative aspects of our lives are exposed.

The tendency to evade moral obligations, to turn to medications, to be overly concerned about self, to be short-tempered—all these are exposed in the raw when we do not have the protective covering which our stronger moments provide. At such times when we open ourselves to God's inflow and God's lordship, he reaches deep into new areas of both our conscious and subconscious selves. He becomes more truly Lord of our lives, and this stands as a defensive bulwark, ready for the next period of emptiness or fatigue.

What do we do with our solitude? Our thoughts can be occupied with gratitude to God or with fantasy flights which inflate our egos through the process of imagination. Our minds may rest on God's goodness or be riddled with fears and forebodings. The solitary hours may find us either aimless and lonely or relaxed and being recreated in readiness for God's next bidding.

One thing is sure: God intends us for fellowship with him. We are made to be his friends. As Saint Augustine discovered, "Our lives are restless until they rest, O Lord, in thee." Each one of us is God's unique child, "called by name" (Isa. 43:1). Each of us is significant to God. He says to each of us, even as he said to Jesus, "You are my beloved son in whom I am well pleased." It is man's part to accept and to respond to this love. "We love him because he first loved us." In responding, we discover a God who relates to us with a love that affirms and challenges us, that bids us both to rest in him and to go forward in his strength.

We often come to God asking for answers to our questions, only to find that he gives us more difficult and deeper questions for us to answer.

Sue turned to God with a broken and bitter heart. "Why did you let my husband die? He was so young, and I need him so much!"

Slowly, God's questions came back to her, "Have you

found the real purpose for living yet? Will you trust your husband to me? Will you give me the rest of your life?"

Sue moved from shallowness to depth, from bitterness to fulfillment, from aimlessness to meaning. Being the kind of Father he is, God pushes us out beyond our depth, widens our horizons, confronts us with problems beyond our solving in order that we may search, trust, and grow.

A requisite for fellowship with God is our willingness to come to him in sincerity and honesty. In the story of the Pharisee and the publican, Jesus tells us that the publican was much more acceptable to God because of his forthright honesty in saying, "God, be merciful to me, a sinner." If we come into God's presence with any known sin which we are unwilling to acknowledge, that sin becomes a barrier. It is like a piece of dirt in an electrical connection which prevents the flow of electrical current and cuts short the power.

The God who heard the cries of the slaves in Egypt and led them from captivity into the Promised Land, and who revealed himself to us in Jesus Christ, is a God who will keep his covenant of friendship with his children. While the Bible tells frequently of man's search for God, it tells even more frequently of God's search for man. "I have loved you with an everlasting love" (Jer. 31:3, RSV).

God always fulfills his part of the fellowship. When our sense of nearness to him fades and we cry out, "O that I knew where I might find him," the fault is always ours, for he is ever taking the initiative toward us. It is we who raise barriers. Whenever we will listen, become willing, and offer him his rightful place as king of our lives, he will enter not only as King but as Father and Friend.

QUESTIONS FOR STUDY

1. You have already taken a moral inventory of your life as you have read this chapter. Now talk over the results of such self-analysis with a group or some one person in whom you have complete trust.

2. Where is your security? In good health? In financial security? In the good opinions of friends? In success in your work? How do these things actually compare with your trust in God?

3. Everyone has the potential to put people into categories that limit or diminish them, or to affirm and enhance them. Do you speak negatively about others—your children, your neighbors, your fellow church members? Do you characterize or pigeonhole people, not allowing for maturing growth or real character changes that have taken place? How can you affirm people?

4. In what direction do you feel that God is pushing you out of the nest and calling you to greater commitment and the assuming of greater responsibilities?

5. Describe the ways in which you ascertain the will of God for yourself.

··{9}··
Meeting God Daily

To start the day with God, and not with problems to be solved, can make a tremendous difference in one's life. Yet many people find that the idea of morning devotions presents an insurmountable problem because they just don't know how to begin. There is no one way that is right for everybody. Each person can discover the manner in which God becomes most real for him. But if you would like to begin the practice of affirming God's presence in your life daily, let me describe the method I use. It may suggest ways in which you can get started.

Thanksgiving. I begin by giving thanks. While showering and getting dressed, I set the mood of the day as one of praise and gratitude. I thank God for this day, both in general and in specifics, silently thinking through or voicing my gratitude for those close to me at home and at work, for the night's rest and the day's strength, for the sheer joy of being alive.

Honesty. There are days when God seems far away, and occasionally I do not even want to meet him. I have no inclination to read my Bible or to pray. Probably, deep in my heart, I do not want to hear—much less obey—what God has to tell me. On these occasions I frankly admit how I feel, that I want nothing to do with him. Sometimes just the verbalization of this thought removes the barrier so that I feel close to him again. Other times, I need to pray until I realize his presence. And there are days when I simply get to work knowing that he is there even though I cannot feel his presence. Most of the time, however, God *is* real and very close.

Concentration. I find a quiet place and a comfortable chair and settle myself so that I am totally present where I am. I give over all distracting thoughts to God, and unless there is something that needs to be done immediately, such as turning off the flame under the kettle or making an essential phone call, I relax in the chair and in the presence of God. I read the Bible (more on this in chaps. 13 and 14) and let it speak to my situation in relevant terms.

Sometimes I read biography—short stories of personal religious experience such as those found in *Faith at Work* magazine, as well as full biographies. Frequently I read or hum through a hymn or two, letting the words speak to my condition.

Listening. Then I have a time of listening. Its length will vary—a minute or so up to ten minutes. During this period of silence, my thinking is guided by the thoughts arising out of my reading, or perhaps dictated by the tasks that face me that day. I ask myself one or two questions that bring me face to face with reality: "Am I totally God's today? Am I thinking big enough—with God's kind of thinking and strategy? Have I been obedient to what he has shown me in the past? If not, what do I plan to do about it? What would Christ have me be or do today, at home and at work? Is there any relationship in my life where God would have me be more loving or understanding?"

If my mind wanders at times, I do not worry about it or berate myself. I simply bring my thoughts back to where they were and continue. However, the wandering thoughts may be God directing me to other lines of thinking. A moment of reflection will let me know whether these thoughts are aimless, avoiding coming to grips with reality and dodging God's will for me, or if they are exploring new pathways of life which God intends me to travel.

During my time of listening, I keep pen and paper at hand. "The faintest ink is better than the strongest memory." Jotting down ideas impresses truth more deeply on me, helps me to see it in a new dimension, and provides something to which I may refer later. Talking over my thoughts with a friend—often my wife—also helps to clarify them.

Intercession. I devote some time to intercessory prayer, thanking God for people, affirming them, lifting them into the light of God's healing and life-giving love. In my imagination I see persons made whole in heart and body. I discipline myself to see them in fellowship with God and with their fellow-men.

My morning devotions end as they began, with thanksgiving and a stance of faith. I believe!

Whether my day holds casual chores such as washing the car, emptying the garbage, or taking my wife on a shopping expedition, or whether it contains counseling sessions, traveling, or a speaking engagement, I seek to approach the day's work with a sense of mission.

I believe that God calls me to the tasks that are mine each day. This sense of vocation prevails whether I am burning trash in the incinerator or helping someone in a divided home to be reconciled to his partner and to find God's plan for his life once again.

Let me confess, however, that I often slip from this sense of high calling. When I do slip, I know it, and I also know the way back. I ask God to show me where I am at fault and to restore my sense of mission. To "do everything as unto the Lord" is my highest daily desire.

During my devotional meditation, hunches or leadings come into my thoughts. Unlike some people, I do not see visions of what I should do, or hear a voice speaking. God relates differently to people according to their various temperaments. I have only what I call hunches or unfolding thoughts or intuitions. Glenn Clark used to tell how thoughts far beyond his native ability came to him when he was still and waiting for God's guidance.

There are mechanical devices which may help to objectify the prayer experience. Frank Laubach said that he often made the presence of Christ felt by placing an empty chair beside his own and picturing it occupied by Christ, to whom he spoke intimately and conversationally. This method made prayer a reality for him; others reject it as artificial. Everyone can find ways to make devotions more meaningful. As one grows and matures spiritually he may try different devices, or discard them altogether. There is no value in a technique unless it produces results of vital fellowship with God. Find the ways best suited to you and use them.

The question is sometimes raised, "Isn't this 'finding the mind of Christ' nothing but a matter of following one's conscience?"

I think not. Conscience is not necessarily a reliable guide. The word *conscience* comes from *con-scio* (literally, to know or learn together). Our minds are influenced by early training, the attitudes of our peers, the circumstances of our daily lives, and many other factors including the theories of our teachers and the comments of editorial writers. What we have "learned together" does not necessarily echo the spirit of Jesus Christ.

If our lives have been yielded to the Master and we are seeking to have in us "the mind of Christ" (Phil. 2:5), our consciences become *that which we are learning together with Jesus Christ.* The more Christ-centered we become, the more our consciences will coincide with the will of God for us. As we grow in Christ, what seemed right ten months or ten years ago may not seem right today. All we can do is live up to the highest we know at the time we make a decision. God will use even our mistakes, especially when they are made with sincerity of purpose.

But what if a deep problem persists and there is real doubt as to God's will in the matter? There are several steps we may take.

Wait, if possible, before making a final decision. Let the problem rest and see if your thinking becomes clarified. If an immediate decision is imperative, play the hunch that seems right at that moment after checking the hunch against what you believe to be the spirit of Christ. Ask yourself, "How would the love of God be expressed in a situation like this?" If there is time, talk and pray it over with someone you trust. Be doubly careful before accepting as God's guidance any leading that causes you to break previous promises or to go counter to your basic responsibilities at home or on the job, for *God invariably seeks to restore and reaffirm in us our primary loyalties.*

The time of meditation should not become a fetish or something in any way unnatural. It should always be flexible under God's leading. A friend of mine whose desk was piled high with work to be done was trying hard to concentrate on his devotions. As his restlessness increased, he cried out, "God, I can't seem to settle down. What shall I do?" The thought came, "Get to work at that desk. I will be with you." Sometimes God's leading is a simple, "Get started at the next thing you have to do."

Many individuals have the capacity to sense God's presence and talk to him during the day's activities, while commuting, doing housework, driving, or gardening. A bit of discipline and practice can turn these into times of rich fellowship, with concentrated listening and receiving God's direction.

The Italian writer Giovanni Guaraschi has given us a delightful example of this in his stories about the priest Don Camillo. To Don Camillo, God is always present, symbolized by the statue of Jesus in his church. He speaks to the statue simply and with unveiled feelings. There is a wonderful honesty about these conversations. The priest hears the quiet voice reply to him. Sometimes he obeys it; sometimes he takes issue with it; sometimes he disregards it! But always he consults his God and then turns quickly to the business of living.

Each of us has something of God's presence with him—the sense of right, the desire to obey the inner voice, the indwelling Christ. To go about our daily tasks, to hear the inner voice and then to obey it is to live. To make our obedience correspond more nearly each day with this inner word is to live confidently, securely, and joyously.

QUESTIONS FOR STUDY

1. How do you keep your devotions? How do you keep close to God as the day wears on?

2. Recall one or two situations in which God has been very near and real to you while doing some of the routine daily tasks. One disciple of Isaac Walton said, "I wouldn't take a million dollars for the thoughts I have while I am quietly fishing." Is your thought-life enriching?

3. When you have an important decision to make, how do you reach the point of making a definite choice?

4. Most people experience periods of dryness when God seems far away. Have you? What did you do? With what result?

5. When we slip and fall back into our old areas of disobedience, we "know the way back." Describe how you found your way back on one of these occasions.

··{ 10 }··
Locked In

A Christian may become "locked in" at the point where his conversion or spiritual awakening began, or at a place where he has achieved a degree of security, success, or comfort. Growth from this point on is apt to proceed very slowly, if at all.

We see this locked in situation in the establishment of today. Those in places of power and influence who have achieved status and security through work and risks taken in the past tend to hold on to what they possess. There may have been a time when they were pioneers, blazing trails. But now they hold back, attempting to preserve the status quo, uneasy in mind because of the fast-moving changes about them.

University authorities, for example, may cling to established curricula, teaching methods, and forms of government rather than institute changes which would diminish their power, shatter their pedagogy, and eliminate curricula which have become enshrined by time.

A labor union finds it easier to protect its white membership than to risk the uncertainties that might follow the admission of men from minority groups.

In the church, a minister may try to bolster his dwindling congregation by introducing methods to restore what used to be twenty-five years ago instead of instituting radical changes in the structure and function of the parish to make it more productive.

The tendency to resist change reaches into all areas of life. There is always a dread of the "new" among those who are well established in the "old." Yet Jesus likened the Kingdom of God to the man "who brings out of his treasure what is new and what is old" (Matt. 13:52, RSV). This is a difficult concept indeed for people who shy away from the growing edge and remain locked in. Threatened by change, they protect their rights and privileges and look fearfully at contemporary changing conditions in the world about them and at the needs of those less fortunate than they.

This condition exists in groups because it is first seen in individuals. A recovered alcoholic, priding himself on his sobriety, may be blind to his need for growth in other areas. A pastor successful in building his church and serving his parishioners may be ignorant of the loneliness of his own family.

I met a man, recently converted, who was constantly speaking of his changed life and seeking to win others to Christ. But he was completely indifferent to the fact that less than a mile from his home there were malnourished children growing up in conditions of appalling poverty. Another man, who had never set foot in church since childhood, suddenly saw the importance of religious education and began to teach a Sunday school class. But he actively opposed the participation by his church in a program to rehabilitate parolees from a nearby state prison.

In the life and teachings of Jesus there is a conserving of the old that is consistent with the inclusion of the new. As our Lord, he calls us to grow constantly, to leave the security of the present, and to risk the insecurity of the future. Meaning is found in motion. To hold onto something too tightly is to crush the life out of it. Every man has a need to move out into unexplored areas of his life—the listener must learn to speak, the compulsive talker to listen. He who is inclined to withdraw must learn to confront, and he who is skilled at attack must learn how to consolidate his gains. The man who controls only his acts must find how to discipline his desires also.

Moreover, to abandon one addiction for another shows no moral growth. The person who stops drinking and doubles his consumption of tobacco has not proved much. Then to substitute pastries and sweets for cigarettes is also a hollow victory. To compensate for disliking one person by loving another inordinately is in reality falling back and losing ground.

This principle, so obvious in the life of an individual, is also clearly seen on a colossal scale. Revolution is in store for the nation that will not face its problems, but sweeps commission reports on crime and violence under the rug and pays little attention to the root causes of social unrest. For a nation or for an individual there is slow death of the soul in boasting of old areas of growth and refusing to make new explorations of the spirit. Flowers and fruit grow on new wood.

Jesus said, "Grow in me and I will grow in you" (John

15:4). Paul listed the fruits of the Spirit as varied qualities of life—love, joy, peace, patience, kindness, goodness, faithfulness, gentleness, and self-control (Gal. 5:22–23). How often we settle for a small fraction of these! We are faithful to our duties but not joyous; self-controlled but not kind; loving but not at peace within ourselves.

Fred was a typical adolescent, fifteen years old, with tousled hair and a freckled face. He was painfully shy and for some time had been harboring silent hostilities toward his mother and an older sister. He yielded his life to Christ, and God gave him a new love for these two members of his family. Quietly, Fred changed his attitude toward them. His mother was happy in the new relationship, and the whole home seemed different. Yet Fred was as withdrawn and shy as ever.

At a weekend conference six months later, he spoke up with great difficulty, scarcely able to find the words. "I believe God wants me to be more forward and stick my neck out. But I'm scared stiff to do it. I'm afraid I'll make too many mistakes, but I've got to try."

Of all that was spoken at that closing conference session, probably no words cost any speaker more or represented a more real commitment to follow Christ. Here was a young man's growing edge. He knew that to move out would be painful and costly, but God's challenge was clear and unmistakable.

God is always nudging us to leave the security of the nest, as a fledgling must when its time has come to fly. He wants us to explore and cultivate new potentials of personal talents and service to our fellow-men. When growth stops, decay sets in. To live is to learn and to grow.

Religion has too long fostered the desire to hold onto

what is good without reaching out for what is better. We have held tightly to our security, concentrated on balancing church budgets, protecting our status. But we have been all too slow to unlock the doors that have kept us imprisoned. Let us be set free!

Jesus calls us to "creative insecurity." He said, "Whoever loses his life . . . shall find it" (Mark 8:35). He asks men and women to move out into new areas of need, of service, and of social engineering. Such involvement is always costly. Paul put it this way, "forgetting what lies behind and straining forward to what lies ahead, I press on" (Phil. 3:13–14, RSV).

A certain physician, secure in a large practice, said, "God has shown me that I must accept responsibility for the spiritual welfare of my patients as well as for their physical well-being." True, he has lost some patients who felt he was meddling where he did not belong. But this has been more than balanced by others who have come to him for help for both body and spirit and have entered into a newness of physical and spiritual health.

A pastor resolved to risk losing his church, which he knew might happen when he led his suburban parishioners to open involvement with black neighbors.

A church-school superintendent saw that the long hours she spent on religious education were in large measure an escape from a difficult husband and complex home situation. Church business had become her substitute for genuine inner growth. She resigned her job and sought to repair the broken relationships within her family.

There is risk in reaching out to the unknown. A man once said to me, "My wife and I live together so peacefully that I hate to risk the tranquillity. But we haven't really talked to each other about our deeper thoughts and emotions for fifteen years. Neither of us knows the other person deep inside."

It is all too comfortable to sit tight and hold on to what we have. God is calling us to relinquish the certain present (which in reality is far from certain) for the uncertain future. He pushes us away from our contentment with what is and seeks to replace it with a divine discontent, a longing for what he yet has to offer.

It is a risky venture. So, also, was the road to Calvary.

QUESTIONS FOR STUDY

1. Read the words of Jesus, "You have heard that it was said . . . but I say to you" (see Matt. 5:21–47). Interpret this saying in terms of these present changing times.

2. Can you think of any secure area in your life which God is asking you to leave and a new one which he is asking you to occupy? As children grow up, as men move to new jobs, as the church faces new tasks in a changing world, etc., how do you feel about these situations? What is God asking you to do about them?

3. We cannot remain stationary, but we must have growing edges in our lives. What is your next step in Christian growth?

4. What tends to hold a person back in safe and secure places? What tends to send a man out into new fields of endeavor and new styles of living? How can you overcome the former and develop the latter?

··{ *11* }··

Companions on the Way

M an is a gregarious animal. From time immemorial he has sought the companionship of his fellows in family groups, hunting parties, tribes. Then, down the corridors of history, he has formed fraternal organizations, guilds, clubs, and all sorts of associations. The urge to belong is natural, for it is quite impossible for man to live in isolation.

There is, however, a very special grouping or relationship that awaits the man who has made his commitment to the way of Christ. John wrote, "If we walk in the light, as he is in the light, we have fellowship [koinonia] with one another" (1 John 1:7, RSV). Koinonia is the Greek word used in the New Testament to describe the deep and joyous fellowship of the early Christians. In such a fellowship, people become increasingly known to one another. They see how much alike they are, cut from the common matrix of humanity. They bear each other's burdens, undergird one another in supportive love and prayer. They have a common and undivided loyalty to their leader, Jesus Christ. They are overwhelmed and amazed at the great love of God who has forgiven and remade them. They are embarked on a common mission—the building of a new world, the Kingdom of God. They stand in awe before the stupendous truth that God in Christ has chosen them to be bearers of the Good News, channels of his love, earthen vessels that contain his treasures.

Jesus himself was a member of a group. He spent a great deal of time with his twelve disciples, opening his heart and laying bare his innermost feelings to them.

Group fellowship, whether within a family, in an informal gathering of friends, or in a more formal setting, can be an enriching experience of learning and maturing. The power of the group undergirds men as they move out into life's arenas of action. They are strengthened and encouraged by the love and prayer of their fellow-men.

There are countless ways to start a group. The most effective group of which I was a part during a fifteen-year pastorate began with two people.

I was new in the parish, and no one really knew the inner me—the lonely battles, the struggle to let faith conquer feelings, the effort to keep my mask off and be real. I longed to be known, even though I dreaded the prospect in some ways. Nevertheless, I needed to have someone who really knew me and could undergird me with supportive prayer and love.

The name of one layman came to mind, and I felt that God wanted me to open my life to him. I both welcomed and feared the idea.

The layman accepted my request to spend an evening with him. I told him of my lonely childhood, my deep feelings of inferiority, my battles with pride and lust, my desire to be praised, my fear of criticism, my nervous breakdowns, my high aspirations and longing to be used by God in building his Kingdom.

Our conversation ended with earnest prayer. I felt that I had found a new friend, on a level deeper than I had dreamed possible. As I rose to go, my friend said, "Will you come back next week?"

"I won't need to," I said. "I came tonight with no axe to grind, no plan to take any more of your time."

"If you would come," he replied, "I'd like to tell you *my* story."

"Forgive me, Bill," I apologized. "How selfish I am, thinking only of my need and desire to be known."

The following week I returned and Bill told me his life story, which throbbed with anguish and drama. We had shared our mutual needs, and our prayers took on new meaning that night as our hearts were knit in deep friendship.

It was the most natural thing that we should meet once a week after that, just the two of us. We studied the Bible together, trying to apply its teachings to our personal situations. Nearly four months passed before a third man, seeing a change in Bill, asked if he could join us. Two months later a fourth was added to our little circle. Then, one by one, ten or twelve others were added.

We met weekly for nearly five years, and the lives of all of us were changed as we grew spiritually. Not only that, the spiritual climate of the entire congregation was deeply affected.

As man is made for fellowship with God, so is he also made for fellowship with his brothers. Teilhard de Chardin writes of a "tendency to cohere" throughout the universe. Man is constantly being reminded of his oneness with his fellow-men. Jesus emphasized our need to love one another. As his Spirit enters a man's life, he begins to have a new compassion for others. He sees the Spirit of God at work in his fellows; he stops sitting in judgment on them and realizes that everyone has something to learn and something to give. He has a growing sense of community.

Single logs don't burn well. If the fire of spiritual vitality is to be kept alive, we must have fellowship. And whatever form the group may take, it is well that its members find time for study both of spiritual principles (primarily from the Bible) and of the world's needs. All study, however, should be relevant to daily life. It is useless to study the life of Jesus or to delve into social problems such as racism, poverty, or war, and let it end with a discussion of ideas or the formulation or defense of a theology. How often we come to the Bible to bolster our ideas rather than to find direction and power for new ways of living! All study should be directed toward our own inner needs and the discovery of potentials issuing in new depth of community with God's people and new attitudes and actions. Groups should generate a genuine zeal for building God's kingdom. If they do not, they may be more of an escape from reality than anything else.

Part of the practice of a group, whether it be just two people or a dozen or more, should be the use of a period of silence. This provides a unique opportunity to consider such questions as these: *Should I be building a closer relationship with someone? Exactly what steps should I take? What is God's next step for me? Where am I holding back? What needs are there in my community that I can help to meet?*

Take a few minutes to wrestle with such questions. Following the period of silence there should be an opportunity for people to open their hearts and speak of the thoughts that came to them, if they are willing to do so.

If one has been meeting with a group and senses that it is losing its effectiveness, he should take the initiative to revitalize it or to recommend that it be disbanded and possibly reformed. Merely to criticize will bring little power to deepen or rebuild a fellowship. To take the initiative in the revitalization of a group may require some changes in the attitude of the individual most concerned.

Here are some practical guidelines that have proved helpful to me over a period of years in my relationship with groups. These guidelines will be especially meaningful to the individual who has taken responsibility to get the group started and/or keep it going.

1. Set the members of the group free to be themselves. Love them as they are. See the good, the Christ in them, already at work in their lives. Be interested in what interests them rather than trying to spark their enthusiasm for your pet ideas and projects. Be sure that you are more intent on genuinely loving them (that is, listening, caring, liking, affirming) than on trying to make them over into small editions of yourself—or what you think they ought to be.

2. Ask two or three members of the group to whom you feel drawn to meet separately with you for prayer and costly openness of heart. Ask God to show you the areas of your lives which are not yet completely his. Are there relationships that need to be made more Christlike?

Search your hearts and see if you genuinely love the other members of the group. In a time of silence together, consider what further steps God would have each of you take, in attitudes as well as in deeds.

3. Be willing to express yourself on a more costly level. Share the struggles that take place deep within your own heart. Tell of any impatience and resentment you have felt with the group or with others. Seek forgiveness. Acknowledge any self-righteousness or judgmentalism you have discerned in yourself, and if others discern it in you, be willing to consider whether they are right before you flare up in self-defense.

4. As a leader of the group, be relaxed, be yourself, but see the potential in each person. Have a purpose or plan for the meeting, but hold to it loosely, for God's Spirit may take the leadership in an entirely different direction. Then, "when something happens, capitalize on the happening."

5. Maintain balance. A group that is at its best should have *depth*, *study*, and *mission*. *Depth* means that each person increasingly trusts himself to the others; he becomes personally more vulnerable, but the fellowship group becomes stronger. *Study* moves largely on the level of ideas, which can keep people at arm's length and inhibit involvement. People do not often reveal their inner selves in a discussion of ideas and concepts. Depth and study, therefore, draw on the emotional and the intellectual self, but not the functional. Without the third thrust of *mission* the group will tend to become ingrown and sterile. Hence the need for the outward movement so that the group may maintain a healthy balance. Mission means serving in places of need, being used to change lives and situations.

Ask yourself if one of these emphases—depth, study, mission—is being overlooked in your group.

6. From time to time, invite people in from outside to share news of what is happening in other groups and communities. It is so easy to become parochial, to ride pet hobbies, to become ingrown and selfish. A new voice can be a fresh breeze of the Spirit.

7. If there is a lack of interest and vitality in the group, ask the members to tell why. Share your own areas of fault, and then invite the others to say what they really want: a deeper quest? a social evening? a group to lean on which will free them from personal initiative and confrontation with God? Or do they perhaps want out?

Consider the wisdom of discontinuing the group. A decent funeral is better than preserving a corpse. Point out the cost and the challenge of a group whose members are willing to be known, trusting themselves to one another and being supported by mutual prayer and love. Face the cost of being in mission, but emphasize the rich rewards and the joy of this style of life. If interest in the group has waned, it may be right to disband and start another group later on.

8. Be willing to break old molds. Some groups work better for limited periods of time—between Labor Day and Christmas, for example, or between New Year and Easter, or between Easter and Memorial Day. Some churches change the composition of their groups each year. Others split their groups annually, each half trying to find an equal number of new members to complete a new group. Feel free to discover the plan, the time, the place of meeting, and the persons involved which are most suitable for your particular requirements.

9. Deal in specifics, whether in prayer or discussion. If someone says, "I want to be more loving," let someone else ask, "Loving to whom? On what particular occasions?" If the statement is made, "I should be a better worker on the job," press the specific, "In what regard? What makes you say this? Will you spell that out in detail?" An observation such as, "I should be a better father," should lead to questions such as, "To which child in particular? What steps do you think God wants you to take to bridge the gap?"

10. Learn how to utilize silence. After costly sharing or some deep insight out of Bible study, suggest a time of "listening" (one to ten minutes, depending on the group's ability to use silence). The leader should then go around the circle, asking what thoughts have come during this quiet time, with little or no comment or discussion. If there are those who do not wish to speak, they should feel free to remain silent. After all who wish to speak have had the opportunity to do so, invite comment and discussion or further sharing. The ideas that emerge from the period of silence may well furnish the group with its "homework" for the week ahead.

11. Pray audibly, briefly, in specifics, and in the first person singular. Try praying around the circle for the person on your left or on your right. Recall what specific concerns have been expressed. Affirm these for one another as specifically as they were revealed. "God, help John to be frank with his son and to talk about his own experiences as a boy his age." "Dear Lord, help Judy to make that apology with real love and forgiveness in her heart."

Vary the ways in which you pray. Try conversational prayer, as outlined by Rosalind Rinker in her book, *Prayer*

—*Conversing with God*. If it seems right, grasp the hand or lay hands on the head of the person being prayed for. Above all, be specific, concrete, and brief.

12. Let each member of the group engage in daily, supportive, specific prayer for each of the other members. There is more power in specific prayers than in generalizations, for there is a greater element of expectancy and faith. This type of prayer often leads to phone calls or conversations during the week. At the next meeting, begin by referring to those goals which were spoken of at the last meeting. In the business world, a board of directors will check up on production and progress since they last met. In like manner, check up lovingly on one another with such questions as: "What happened this week between you and Gene?" "Have you had that cup of coffee with your neighbor yet?" Be specific. Pin it down.

13. There is no substitute for genuine interest and concern, for loving people as they are and setting them free to grow at their own pace under the leading of the Holy Spirit. With love should go a genuine honesty. Friendships can easily become phoney if we present a "holy" or "beautiful" image in order to impress people. We can easily say things to produce an effect, to get people to think or act in our way. Let us rather be both loving and "for real."

14. Ask the members of the group to consider the purpose of its existence. Why are they meeting? What do they expect to happen? Are they willing to accept these goals:

Each person willing to trust himself more and more to the group and to prove increasingly trustworthy as he comes to know the others. Each person to be drastically honest with himself and lovingly honest with others.

Each person to find God's will, and his own place in the building of God's Kingdom, starting in his own life, his own home, and beyond as far as God may guide.

Each person to move forward to a deeper and total (as far as he can see at the moment) commitment to Jesus Christ.

Specialists in group dynamics say, "The answer is always in the group." This is especially true of a fellowship group in Christ. When we interrelate in openness and costly love, the Holy Spirit is present, and "He will guide you into all the truth" (John 16:13, RSV).

QUESTIONS FOR STUDY

1. Which of the guidelines for revitalizing groups are relevant for your groups? Where can you begin? What can you do?

2. Are there any further steps you could take to weld your group more closely together, whether the family group, prayer group, business group, board of deacons, etc.?

3. What do you see as the most essential elements in a productive group? What is the sequence of importance?

4. Which element or elements are missing in your group that would add considerably to its fellowship and effectiveness? What can you do about this?

5. Describe some particular group experience that made a deep impression on you and resulted in a change in your style of life.

..{*12*}..

Breaking Bread Together

I t was Sunday, the final day of the weekend renewal conference, and four hundred people had gathered in the
hotel ballroom early in the morning for a sacramental
meal. I had been asked to conduct this service, and I looked
out over the crowd of men and women, seated around
tables in groups of ten. In the center of each table was a
glass of grape juice and a bread roll, similar to those served
at our regular meals.

After we had sung a couple of hymns, I asked each
group of ten to appoint a leader. This was to be the person
whose birthday was closest to April 11, the date of the
following Easter. I then asked everybody to learn the first
names of his table-mates. There was a quiet buzz as each
group determined their leader and memorized names. We
then sang a chorus:

Spirit of the Living God, fall afresh on me.
Melt me, mold me, fill me, use me.

Surveying the crowd from my position at the podium,
I realized that at least one quarter of the people had their

backs to me; yet it seemed right for each person to be facing his table-mates, identifying with his circle of ten rather than with the larger group. After a prayer of gratitude to God, we claimed by faith the presence of our risen Lord as we were about to partake of the elements before us.

I spoke about the meal two thousand years ago when Jesus said good-by to his disciples, and we sensed the good-bys we would be saying to one another in a few hours. "The miracle of that good-by was that Christ would still be with them. As often as they broke bread together, he was there."

We now claimed the greater miracle that the risen Christ was there with us. The grape juice and bread were symbols of his presence. This service was not only a memorial, but a celebration of the fact of his presence among us.

Taking up one of the rolls, I broke it, speaking of the brokenness in the heart of Jesus. "He did not come to lord it over us, but humbled himself, becoming vulnerable. He was pushed around, thrown out of his hometown, spat upon, mocked, and nailed to a cross in a public spectacle of disgrace and futility.

"We can partake of this meal as a ceremony or ritual which we perform by habit—our bodies present, doing everything in proper decorum—or we can bring our entire beings into the presence of the Master."

As we were about to sing again the chorus, "Melt me, mold me, fill me, use me," I spoke of my own need to be melted and molded. "There is in me something that resists change. I still want to do things my way. I would like to be filled and used on my terms, rather than have God make me over into his mold."

Quietly came the challenge: "Where are the places of your resistance? At what point is your pride unwilling to be broken and humbled? What are the things you've said you'll 'never do'? What are the steps that for a long time the Master has been asking you to take?

"Let us sing the chorus again, and when we come to those four verbs, let us think in specifics. 'Where does God want to melt me? Where am I rigidly refusing to change? In what fashion does he want to mold me? Where am I resisting? I am asking him to fill me, but if I am already filled with anxiety, fear, and self-will, with plans for my life, there is no room for him. Am I willing to be emptied in order to be filled? Am I ready to be used in any way, at any time he wishes?"

A period of silence followed while we thought of places where God wanted us to be different.

"Suppose the risen Christ took over your life completely. What changes would occur? In the silence think in terms of specifics, not generalities."

The moments of soul-searching past, I suggested that we all pray aloud, beginning with the leader at each table and going around the circle to the right, using this formula, "I leave at this table . . .", specifying what each one intended to give over to Christ at this moment.

"Limit your prayer to one sentence. Be specific. Don't just say, 'I leave my pride,' but specify the area of pride. If anyone believes he should not pray aloud, let him feel free to be silent, touching his neighbor when it is his turn as an indication of his desire to pass."

The room hummed with the subdued voices of men and women emptying themselves before God.

When everyone had prayed, the leader at each table took the bread, broke off a small piece, and passed it to the neighbor on his right, addressing him by his first name and saying, "This is the body of Jesus Christ, broken for you." The neighbor in turn broke off a piece of bread and passed on the roll and the greeting.

This done, I took up a glass of grape juice. "Of this cup Jesus said, 'This is my blood of the covenant, which is poured out for many for the forgiveness of sins.' Jesus was celebrating the Passover with his disciples. This paschal feast originated in Egypt as the Israelites prepared for a journey to the Promised Land. Their celebration was an act of faith that they would truly be delivered from bondage and enter into Canaan.

"Today, by faith in Christ, we celebrate deliverance from sin and our entrance into the fellowship of the victorious people of God. Ours is also an act of faith that God has delivered us and goes with us on our journey. Our lives are to be a continuous appropriation of Christ's indwelling presence and a love for our fellow Christians as we walk daily into the unknown with him.

"He has said of this cup, 'This is my blood.' 'Blood' and 'life' are synonymous; to lose one is to lose the other. To give blood for a brother by transfusion is to give life. For Jesus to shed blood for us meant to give life to us. Deuteronomy 12:23 puts it this way: 'The blood is the life.' Therefore, in drinking of this cup, by faith we are taking the life of Christ into our lives. It is a spiritual transfusion of divine plasma into our inmost beings.

"As we come to him this morning in our brokenness, he gives us his wholeness. For our emptiness he offers his fulness; for our anemic weakness, his full-blooded strength; for our inconstant love, his steadfast love; for our selves, his own Self!"

In an attempt to make the ceremony more vividly meaningful, I used the following illustration: "The philosopher Schopenhauer described the plight of a group of porcupines marooned one bitter cold night in the middle of a large, frozen field. There was no escape from the biting wind. They could not burrow into the frozen ground. As they huddled together to keep warm, their sharp quills began to prick and hurt. The closer they moved together, the more the pain increased. Some of the animals could not bear the pain, and drew apart to sleep alone. In the morning they were frozen and dead. Those that remained in the pack still lived.

"The cost to the Master of drawing close to his fellowmen was the shedding of blood. He calls us to this fellowship. Every time we draw close to one another there can be pain. We cease to bless when we cease to bleed. But he who follows his Master knows both the pain and the joy of fellowship. We must learn to live together or we shall die in our aloneness.

"A few moments ago we renounced those things that fettered us and were displeasing to God. This left a vacuum that Christ in his bounty can fill. Let us be silent before we drink, thanking God for all that he is offering us.

"What bounties he has spread out before you—his forgiveness, love, joy, selflessness, awareness of others, willingness to listen to your children, willingness to have dialogue with those whom you have avoided. God offers you his very self in the form of the indwelling Christ."

Each leader now took the glass and a napkin, this time

greeting the person on his left, "This is the blood, the very life of Jesus, being offered for you, Helen." And so the cup passed around the table as each one was addressed by name, took a sip of the juice, and conveyed the greeting to his neighbor.

Again there were two minutes of silence, and then I said, "Let the leader start the sentence prayers as before, this time going to the left, using the formula: 'I take from this table . . .' Let each one mention specifically what he is receiving by faith from God as he prays."

The room was filled with many voices, but with one Spirit as we sensed God's presence in a very real way. When all had prayed, I asked them to rise and sing the fourth verse of the hymn, "Christ the Lord Is Risen To-day."

Soar we now, where Christ has led;
Following our exalted head;
Made like him, like him we rise;
Ours the cross, the grave, the skies. Alleluia!

When the hymn had been sung, we "passed the peace" in this way: the person to the right of the leader at each table held his hands, palms together, toward the leader, who clasped the outstretched hands in his own, calling the person by name and affirming for him what he had prayed for. "The tenderness of Christ be yours in your home, Jim." "Jim" then turned to his right to clasp the hands of his neighbor and affirm him, and so on around the circle.

New meaning and vitality had been brought to an old ceremony. The ritual had come alive. The presence of Christ was mediated through the elements of the meal as we prayed in specific terms with and for one another.

Honesty had bound individuals to each other and to God. We felt that we had been knit together in community— the Body of Christ. The life of God had suddenly broken in upon the life of man. The meal had truly been a celebration of his presence. And the spoken benediction was not an ending but a sending, as we went out each on his own journey with the risen Lord.

Questions for Study

1. Do you tend to fear the "new," especially changes in familiar rituals and habits of religion and worship? Can you recall an introduction of a new form of worship that has been a helpful experience to you?

2. Do you find witnessing the sacrament of baptism and partaking of the Lord's Supper to be largely a matter of habit? Or do you bring your total self to be present at the sacraments? What changes are effected in you as you participate?

3. How do you use the silence during the Lord's Supper? What is the substance of your prayers? What are the kinds of thoughts that go through your mind?

4. Describe a communion service that meant a great deal to you. Why?

5. Try an informal fellowship meal once a month at your own family table using some of the ideas in this chapter, using a roll and milk, or bread and coffee. Try it in your group. Share with your group what it meant to you.

··{ *13* }··

The Bible Comes Alive

The late Quentin Warner, a Canadian clergyman whose life and witness were powerfully used by God with many people, once said that after he had dedicated his life to Jesus Christ, the Bible and Prayer Book became new books for him.

"The words of the Bible leaped out of the page at me," he said. "They were alive! The words of the staid old Prayer Book got up and walked around the room. Everything became new.

"Until then Bible characters had been like saints in stained-glass windows, pious and apart. Now they became alive, real persons who stepped down from their pedestals, walked the aisles of the church, and came and sat down beside me."

At the time I heard Quentin Warner say this, I discounted it as the work of an overactive imagination. Yet deep in my heart I wished that it might be true. And in time it did indeed become true for me.

The Bible is made up of printed words, originally, hand-written words. Before it was written, however, it was lived. Abraham, Moses, Hosea, Jesus, and Paul were historical personages. Their lives were living words. And Jesus' life was in a unique way the living Word of God—the Word become flesh. Two thousand years ago, the will or word of God was embodied in the living person of a carpenter named Jesus. The Bible contains the record of God alive in other men, too—men who were God's living word and about whom we can now read on the printed page.

This alone is fantastic—to know that God was once alive in the flesh, that he is not only a God *of* history but also a God *in* history, living and working through human beings. Supremely so through Jesus! The Bible would be a great book if this were all that it recorded—the mighty acts of God, made known to us in and through men of passions like our own.

Even more fantastic is the fact that as I read of what happened in those men, something stirs deep in my heart suggesting that I, too, can be like them. What they were *then*, I am called to be *now*. It is something like a duck waddling in the barnyard, hearing the call of the migrating wild ducks as they wing their way northward. A strange stirring within tells him he belongs high up there, not down below, picking up hand-scattered corn. Instinctively he wants to join the others in their flight.

The various parts of the Bible were written, gathered together, and preserved so that these miracles might happen again. The function of Scripture reading, as of liturgy and the sacraments, is to produce this kind of identification. It is to present an encounter that will effect a response and change in our life style.

The Gloria Patri sums it up: "As it was, is now, and ever shall be." Abraham's faith, Moses' bold leadership, the suffering love of Hosea, Paul's newness of heart—these can all be rediscovered and experienced again and again. Historical events reported in the Bible were not majestic terminals but exciting models to be repeated in the current situation. What happened then can happen again, now, in each one of us who believes!

Peter, preaching on the day of Pentecost, said, "This is that which was spoken by the prophet Joel; . . . saith God, I will pour out of my Spirit upon all flesh: . . . your young men shall see visions, and your old men shall dream dreams" (Acts 2:16–17, KJV). In effect, Peter was saying, "What we see happening now is what Joel foresaw."

It is equally true that when we see miracles of awakened men and changed lives today we can say, "This is that which happened in New Testament times. As it was then, so it is now." Reading the printed page can so set us aflame that once again the word can by faith become alive in us. Thus the cycle is complete. The written word—originally a living word—has become a living word once more!

For years I had been in the habit of reading the Bible for two purposes—to prepare sermons or Bible expositions and to enrich my devotional life. I was under no illusion that one could substitute for the other. I knew full well that I might prepare a moving sermon or an interesting Bible study and yet hold onto some area of self-will that I would not give over to God.

One of the talks on which I received more than the usual number of favorable comments was delivered at a Good Friday service shortly after I had spoken quite sharply and cruelly to my wife. Many parishioners said how much that talk had helped them, but my soul was in hell. To this day I remember the flattering words that bolstered me in my sin! Of course the compliments were sincere, but I turned them into a place of refuge where I could hide from my failure.

All that day I remained stubborn. Saturday was Black Saturday and I slept poorly that night. Finally, I could live with myself no longer, and about four-thirty on Easter morning I awakened my wife and told her of the black mass of stubborn resentment in my heart. I asked her forgiveness, and she gave it.

I don't remember whether the sermon I preached later that morning was any good. I only recall now the joy of a heart set free.

It violates the spirit of Scripture to approach the Bible looking for verses to defend a point of view or to bolster existing beliefs or theological positions. To do this is not only to misuse the Bible, but to inhibit new ideas and growth in ourselves. The Bible is not a compendium of arguments, but a gateway to the presence of God, to be read for itself and for the resultant communion with God.

In those moments of solitary contemplation when we read Scripture and meditate upon it, or later, in those "idle moments" when what we have read comes back into our consciousness, new insights will come, new depths will be revealed, and new areas will be unfolded where we need to strengthen existing relationships or build new ones. Thus we do not seek to bolster or embroider the old, but stand firmly on what has been given as we reach out into the new with the ever-ongoing Christ.

I must also come to the Bible with a heart yielded to

God, willing to be obedient, unlike my attitude that Good
Friday when I was too stubborn to obey. The great breakthrough in my life came thirty-seven years ago when for
the first time I was willing to be honest with my fellow-
men, starting with my wife and moving on to members of
my congregation and others. The very next time I read
my Bible the words took on new meaning. They gleamed
and sparkled with reality. Obedience was the key to opening the Scriptures.

The Bible calls into being my uniqueness. It does not
make me conform or seek to copy someone else—not even
Jesus in the sense of trying to duplicate what he did. Scripture speaks to the person deep within myself, affirming
me and my infinite worth in God's eyes.

Bible stories speak to me in two ways. First, they convict me of my failures and ineffective ways of living. They
really "club" me. As I read the early chapters of Genesis,
I am Adam. I see myself made of dust, earthy, running
and hiding from my deeds and from my Maker. I, too,
have been Cain, acting cruelly to my brother man. I too
have built my futile towers of Babel.

And I see myself in Moses, afraid to stand before Pha-
raoh; in Achan's secretiveness as he hid the stolen goods;
in David as he lusted for Bathsheba; in James and John as
they asked for the best seats in heaven; in Peter as he deserted and denied his Master in the critical hour of need.
The Bible cuts me to size. I stand convicted in its presence.
I have no words but, "God be merciful to me, a sinner." I
pray again David's prayer: "Have mercy upon me, O
God, . . . Create in me a clean heart, . . . and renew a
right spirit within me" (Psalm 51:1, 10, KJV).

But if the Bible convicts me, it also assures me of forgiveness. I know that as I confess my sin to God, as I make restitution to my fellow-men, as I sincerely repent and start obediently to walk in a new way of life, God does indeed forgive and fill me with his Spirit.

Yes, the same Book that convicts also affirms. When I read its pages, again and again I find myself saying, "This is the kind of person I can be. This is for me. I too can have this power; this joy is mine also. I too am Christ's disciple; he is sending me out. I feel his call. He gives me his blessing and his power."

Jesus looked deep into Simon's life, below and beyond the boastful, talkative fellow that others saw, and perceived the potential "Rock" that Peter could become. The same Jesus looks into my life and sees a potential that I never dreamed was there. He says to me, as to everyone, "You, too, are God's son. I see untold worth in you." To doubt this is to doubt the God who made us. "Follow me," says our Lord, "and I will give you 'power to become' the person you can be."

The Bible assures us that in Christ we are children of the King, made in the image of God. Eternity is in our hearts. We are heirs to all of God's treasures, joint heirs with Jesus Christ. With Christ in our lives, we can walk erect with the same assurance he had when he said, "I am the way; I am the resurrection; I am the living water." In like spirit, each of us can say, "I am a child of God. I can do all things through Christ who strengthens me."

The world may surround us with formidable opposition, yet we can say like Martin Luther, "Here I stand. God helping me, I can do no other."

In times of uncertainty, confusion, and deep involvement with life's problems, we can say, "This I know:

nothing can separate me from the love of God." Wars and riots may be rampant, but we live in hope and confidence of God's ultimate victory. We too can lay down our lives in the battle for justice and freedom and the brotherhood of man, knowing that he has in store for us the resurrection.

QUESTIONS FOR STUDY

1. Is the Bible a book filled with helpful, beautiful, familiar verses, or do its words come alive so that you feel *they are meant for you?* Mention some verses that really "turn you on."

2. Recall and describe some incident when the barrier between you and some fellow-man kept the Bible from having meaning for you. Or recall a verse that, quite unexpectedly, seemed to take on new meaning in a problem situation or led toward a restitution and healing of some unhappy relationship.

3. Who is your favorite Bible character? Why?

4. What is a favorite Bible passage? Why?

5. What passage leaves you most uncomfortable? Why?

6. What passage gives you strength and confidence? Why?

7. Try reading, at one sitting, various modern translations of the same chapter or incident, comparing them with the familiar King James Version. Experience the new depths and insights such reading can bring to old, long familiar passages.

..{*14*}..

Steps in Bible Study

This is the story of one man's method of Bible study. There are many different ways to approach the Scriptures. Some people choose favorite passages and dwell largely on them. Others select a topic or theme, such as grace, faith, salvation, and trace it throughout the various books of the Bible. Still others see the Scriptures in basically historical terms, studying the acts of God in human life and his unfolding purposes. It is also possible to choose a biographical method, concentrating on personalities—the prophets, David, Peter, Paul, and especially Jesus.

Many people study the Bible one book at a time. I try to read the New Testament all the way through at least once a year, meanwhile paying particular attention to one book, "camping" in the heart of it for two or three months. But I have derived the greatest benefit from Bible study by approaching any passage with these four steps in mind: *understand, personalize, apply,* and *obey.*

Understand. To grasp the essential meanings of the Bi-

133

ble poses great difficulties for many individuals. Repeated reading will often clarify familiar passages, and yet there may remain sections which seem to be impenetrable.

For example, the Book of Revelation, parts of Daniel, and some other isolated chapters still puzzle me and leave unanswered questions. Revelation and Daniel are both examples of apocalyptic writing which poses insuperable difficulties to many contemporary people. While I read these books occasionally, I do not worry about what I cannot understand in them. The parts of the Bible that give me concern are those that I *do* understand. I am quite sure what these passages mean. "Love your enemies. . . . overcome evil with good . . . speaking the truth in love . . . if you are offering your gift at the altar, and there remember that your brother has something against you, leave your gift there before the altar and go; first be reconciled to your brother, and then come and offer your gift" (Matt. 5:44; Rom. 12:21; Eph. 4:15; Matt. 5:23, 24). My main difficulty is not the inability to *understand* such words, but to *obey* them.

Commentaries, Bible study classes, and a knowledge of ancient customs are very helpful. But for the most part, the Bible can be understood when we really want to hear what it is saying.

The Scriptures should be read like any great literature, with the effort to find out what we can about the authors, to get their points of view and purposes in writing. Let us imaginatively re-create the situations described and enter into each incident, seeing it from within the mind of the writer and from the point of view of each participant in turn.

Personalize. Nearly half a century ago, at Lawrence

College in Wisconsin, I was shown a new way to read the Bible. Miss Pearson, a YWCA national secretary, took 1 Corinthians 13:4–8, and asked us students to put the first personal pronoun in the place of the word "love." The passage then read, "I am patient and kind; I am not jealous or boastful; I am not arrogant or rude. I do not insist on my own way; I am not irritable or resentful; I do not rejoice when others go wrong, but rejoice in the right. I bear all things, believe all things, hope all things, endure all things. My love never ends."

To this day I cannot read those verses in this way without being cut to size. I feel bankrupt on every count. But this is anticipating the next step. Suffice it for now to note that what might have remained for me a beautiful reverie on love, or a series of sweet platitudes, suddenly became a quiver of fiery darts that penetrated my inmost being. I am not left ruminating on the beauties of love; I am walking down the empty corridors of my soul, facing ugly shortcomings and memories.

For example, if I read the story of Jesus healing the leper (Mark 1:40–45), I become the leper. Leprosy, I know, causes the extremities of the body to become numb and insensitive, then to decay and fall away. It is "death on the installment plan." By personalizing the story, I see that my life can grow daily more insensitive to people's needs, to the loneliness of my own family or of people in my parish, to the hungry in the world, to the conditions in a jail a few miles away, to murder in the streets of New York City or in a remote village in Vietnam.

Daily, then, I too am dying and need to come to Jesus "beseeching him and kneeling" and saying, "If you will, you can make me clean."

But I may also try to put myself in Jesus' place and personalize that aspect of the story. Merely to see ourselves as the leper can diminish and discourage us. In this connection, I have heard people say that Peter is their favorite Bible character. They can easily relate to him because he is so human, always blundering and slipping. But these people always refer to the Peter before Pentecost, not to the courageous, post-Pentecost Peter who was filled with God's Spirit. Why are we so slow to claim the highest for ourselves?

Therefore, in my imagination I see myself playing Jesus' part. God has sent me, his child, into the world to be a fount of healing, a channel of love, a center of joy. I am to be the hands and feet of this God who would become incarnate again in me. He has no other hands but yours and mine with which to bless this world; no other feet than ours to go where he would go; no other eyes but ours with which to smile on this world; no other hearts than ours with which to love his children everywhere.

A word of caution must be added. In personalizing Bible stories, be sure that you are not so intent on following a technique or pattern that you fail to relax and give yourself over to the happening that God has for you. We can easily get locked into a procedure and block the breeze of the Spirit. By striving to bring about something of our own design, we may become unaware of what God has in store for us.

Apply. Personalizing lends itself to the drastic application of biblical truths. Reading those verses in 1 Corinthians 13, for example, cuts to the quick. As you read them, is it too painful to tarry in their presence and take moral inventory? Can you stop to write down under each of those sixteen statements an incident where you have been convicted of failure? Will you further pray, "My Father, what do you want me to do about this . . . and this . . . and this?"

The late Sam Shoemaker spoke of the Holy Spirit as the "Discomforter" as well as the Comforter. At times the Bible is certainly a discomforting book. Of course, it is easy to read Scripture in search of verses that defend or support a position or doctrine. It is also satisfying to gain historical perspective and to feel that we are growing intellectually. "Yes, I know my Bible," we may say, and quote passage after passage.

But the Bible does not become real until we let God's Spirit say to us with the condemning words of the prophet Nathan, "Thou art the man" (2 Sam. 12:7). The Bible should speak to our condition and to the condition of our churches in terms relevant to life today. It should "match us with this hour," showing us both that we need to be changed and that we are God's chosen people to fulfill his purposes in the world.

To apply the Scriptures drastically to our needs means that we also hear God's words of forgiveness, strengthening, affirmation. We have not let the Bible speak in its entirety until we have heard God saying to us personally, "I have chosen you . . . fear not, for I am with you, be not dismayed, for I am your God; I will strengthen you, I will help you, I will uphold you with my victorious right hand" (Isa. 41:9, 10, rsv).

And to each of us he says, "Thou art my beloved son; with thee I am well pleased" (Mark 1:11, rsv). I was well into middle age before I realized that these great words of loving affirmation spoken to Jesus were meant for me also. Brought up in a loveless home, my parents separated when I was ten, faced with a demand for constant perfection, I developed the worst kind of inferiority feelings. I could not believe that I was precious to God, that he loved me and depended on me to do some special work that he had in mind just for me. But when I accepted the wonder of God's love for me, imperfect as I felt myself to be, the floodgates opened. I saw that God affirms me as he does everyone else who will accept his word and come into his presence with a believing heart.

The Bible is addressed to and meant for the people (laos) of God—the covenant community promised to Abraham, the Kingdom of God emphasized in the teachings of Jesus, the koinonia fellowship groups established by Paul. All who are committed to Christ are the people of God. They are the Church, the Body of Christ.

Scripture helps to draw these people into ever closer fellowship with Christ and with one another, to make them a light, a city on a hill, yeast to leaven the world. Does the reading of God's Word confirm you as a member of the people of God, convict you of the need for closer fellowship, lead you to seek, with this fellowship, strategies for community and world change?

Obey. We should always come away from Bible study with an attitude of expectant faith. If it leaves us discouraged or oppressed, we have wrongly read it. We should not rise from our devotions like driven animals, or condemned doers of duty, but free men, forgiven, redeemed, empowered, and ready for great things.

Again let me emphasize that reading the Scriptures

should not end merely with new ideas, nor even with decisions only. We can get much emotional release and satisfaction from insights and decisions, but these by themselves are of little value. "The road to hell is paved with good intentions." Our reading should carry us through to obedience and action.

To speak of faith in the biblical sense is also to speak of deeds. In both the Old and New Testaments, the concept of faith comprises the dual aspects of belief and action, of surmise and performance. In Hebrews 11:8 we read, "By faith Abraham went out." Faith without action is inconceivable to Hebrew thought. In the western mind, faith can signify entertaining an idea or belief in a creed or doctrine, but the men of the Bible translated their faith into action.

Not long ago my friend Bill Parsons, a pastor in Chelmsford, Massachusetts, wrote to me: "How many joys we find in obedience! You see, love impels us to be obedient. The moment we disobey—one hasty temper, one word not said, one moment of dishonesty with God or our fellowmen, one moment of unloving to wife or children—we have blocked the wonderful flow of his love."

Joyous obedience opens the doors to new insights of God's will. It keeps God's word alive in us. We walk with leaden feet when our hearts are slow to obey.

The story of the Prodigal Son gives us a clear-cut example of this kind of obedience. The Prodigal comes home without any preconditions. He is ready to renounce his right of sonship and become a slave. He abandons all self-claims when he throws himself on his father's mercy. One sees here a complete readiness to accept and to obey whatever is the father's will. The result is that the overflowing love of the father, which had always been available to the son, is now received without measure. The son has obeyed, and the father's love and joy have flooded his heart.

Genuine obedience is often costly, but it is accompanied by joy. The writer of Hebrews said of Jesus, "For the joy that was set before him he endured the cross" (Heb. 12:2).

Let us not fall into the trap of thinking that obedience always involves doing distasteful and unpleasant things. God's will is often a call to do something delightful. An earnest Christian once commented dolefully, "I always recognize God's will when there is something difficult that I don't want to do." What a pathetic misunderstanding!

The call to obey may be a call to play or to rest. One night I returned home late, utterly exhausted after several days on the road. I had been so busy that day that I had taken no time to pray or to read my Bible. Feeling guilty, I tried in vain to get into a mood of prayer.

My wife observed this and said, "God knows you're tired. He knows you've spent yourself in his service. He understands your every thought and emotion. I will get you some warm milk. After that, lie down and relax. Rest your heart in God's everlasting arms and let him restore your spirit." At that moment, God's call for me was simply to "be still" and relax in his love.

Understanding the Bible satisfies the demands of intelligence and common sense.

Personalizing the Scriptures penetrates man's deep inner need for identification, recognition, and affirmation as a person and as a member of the community of God.

Applying keeps biblical insights and injunctions relevant to daily life. It brings man face to face with life's situational experiences and face to face with Eternal Reality.

Obeying marshals all of man's powers in joyous, unified purpose under Christ. The man who gives his all for Christ and his Kingdom truly finds himself. He has embarked on life's most exciting adventure.

QUESTIONS FOR STUDY

1. Describe the method of Bible study that is most productive for you. Do you vary your pattern?

2. Discuss one or two passages of the Bible that are easy to understand but difficult for you to obey.

3. When you have put your name or situation into passages of Scripture, which one has come to mean the most to you? Why?

4. Some persons have a difficult time accepting, as meant for them, the affirmations of the Bible (such as Mark 1:11). Some find it difficult to feel conviction of sin (such as Luke 18:13). Which has been your experience?

5. Do you find a tendency to go to the Bible for ideas and theological insights, but not for power to effect a change in your style of living? Talk about this.

6. How does *obedience* to God's Word contribute to your understanding of the Bible?

Afterword

Let us read those verses from First Corinthians a final time, now putting *Christ* in place of the word *love*.

"The living Christ, who by faith now lives in my life, is patient and kind; this Christ is not jealous or boastful; He is not arrogant or rude. The Christ in me does not insist on his own way; He is not irritable or resentful. The indwelling Christ does not rejoice when others go wrong, but rejoices in the right. The Christ in me bears all things, believes all things, hopes all things, endures all things. Christ's love in me never ends."

When we take the leap of faith, we receive the indwelling Christ into our own lives. He becomes our traveling companion on the way. "All that is past is prologue." With him we walk with confidence into the unknown.

Enjoy the Journey